ENGLISCH IM BERUF

W0209876

English for Legal Professionals

Andrew Frost

SHORT COURSE
SERIES

Cornelsen

Verfasser Andrew Frost, Berlin

Der Autor dankt Hanene Neji, Dr. Albert Kitzler, Andreas Poetke, Roger Wintzer, Claudia Albrecht und Kristi Decke für ihren fachlichen Rat.

Kritische Durchsicht John-Derek Cole, Hannover; Sonia Gwilliam, Hamburg; Victoria Sheppard, Wuppertal; Camilla Woolf, Berlin

Verlagsredaktion Gary S. Helft
Redaktionelle Mitarbeit Oliver Busch (Wortliste), Andrew Fynn, Rebecca Syme
Bildredaktion Uta Hübner
Gesamtgestaltung und technische Umsetzung Sylvia Lang

Quellen *Titelfoto:* F1online/Fancy
Fotos: Fontshop: S. 48, 58, 61, 69; Shutterstock: S. 5 (2), 7, 18, 22, 23, 37 (3), 49, 55, 65; Sony Deutschland GmbH: S. 33; Getty images: S. 43/Ed Honowitz; Masterfile: S. 5, 13, 16, 25, 26; Picture Alliance: S. 37/Bildagentur Huber, S. 46/dpa
Illustrationen: Miriam Elze, Hamburg
Symbole: Andreas Terglane, Kassel

Texte: Beck'sches Formularbuch Zivil-, Wirtschafts- und Unternehmensrecht von Robert Walz (erschienen 2007 im Verlag C.H. Beck, München): S. 51, 56, 61; Cultural Foundation: S. 44–45, 72, 77 (Quoted with kind permission from Cultural Foundation, England. www.cultfound.org); DIHK: S. 14; Epigenomics AG: S. 17; Office of Public Sector Information: S. 65/Guide for Creditors (www.insolvency.gov.uk – Reproduced under the terms of the Click-Use Licence); Pearson Education Ltd: S. 38; Source Media Inc.: S. 57/ Mergers & Acquisitions, January 2008; The Times, London: S. 15/1.12.2003/19.11.2006, S. 25/13.3.2003, S. 36/8.6.2004, S. 46/26.3.2008, S. 47/18.10.2007, S. 68/29.12.2006

Weitere Titel in der *Short Course Series*:

English for Accounting	ISBN 978-3-464-20480-1
English for the Automobile Industry	ISBN 978-3-464-20479-5
English for Customer Care	ISBN 978-3-464-01882-8
English for Emails	ISBN 978-3-464-20007-0
English for the Energy Industry	ISBN 978-3-464-20385-9
English for Human Resources	ISBN 978-3-464-20481-8
English for Marketing and Advertising	ISBN 978 -3-464-01876-7
English for Meetings	ISBN 978-3-464-01874-3
English for Presentations	ISBN 978-3-464-01875-0
English for Real Estate	ISBN 978-3-464-20006-3
English for Sales and Purchasing	ISBN 978-3-464-20225-8
English for Socializing and Small Talk	ISBN 978-3-464-20156-5
English for Telephoning	ISBN 978-3-464-01873-6

www.cornelsen.de

1. Auflage, 1. Druck 2008

Alle Drucke dieser Auflage sind inhaltlich unverändert und können im Unterricht nebeneinander verwendet werden.

Druck: CS-Druck CornelsenStürtz, Berlin

ISBN 978-3-464-20386-6

Inhalt gedruckt auf säurefreiem Papier aus nachhaltiger Forstwirtschaft.

Table of contents

Vorwort

English for Legal Professionals vermittelt Rechtsanwälten und Rechtsberatern sowie Anwalts- und Notariatsgehilfen die notwendigen sprachlichen Mittel, um sich präzise und stilistisch korrekt – mündlich wie schriftlich – in allen Situationen ihres beruflichen Alltags auszudrücken.

Sechs Units decken ausgewählte wesentliche Gebiete des *Commercial Law* ab: Gesellschaftsrecht, Arbeitsrecht, Vertragsrecht, Patent- und Urheberrecht, Übernahme- und Fusionsrecht, Risiko-Management und Insolvenzrecht.

Jede Unit folgt ihrer eigenen Storyline, die interessante Rechtsfragen aufwirft und den bereits erfahrenen Rechtsbeistand bei der Beratung des englischsprachigen Mandanten in die Lage versetzt, die jeweils angemessene rechtliche Vorgehensweise zu wählen: Nachdem der Rechtsbeistand den Mandanten bei der Firmengründung berät (Unit 1), werden Mitarbeiter beschäftigt und Arbeitsverträge ausgehandelt (Unit 2) sowie Verträge mit Handelspartnern (Unit 3) abgeschlossen. Erfolgreiche Firmen lassen ihre Produkte schützen (Unit 4), einige sind in der Lage, kleinere Firmen zu übernehmen (Unit 5); andere müssen sich ihre Risiken näher anschauen, weil sie vielleicht vor der Insolvenz (Unit 6) stehen. Trotz dieses logischen Aufbaus lassen sich die Units auch in beliebiger Reihenfolge voneinander bearbeiten.

Die **Preamble**, eine Aufwärmübung, stimmt auf die thematischen Inhalte jeder Lerneinheit ein und fordert den Lerner auf, vorhandenes Wissen aufzufrischen. Durch die Analyse authentischer Dokumente wird neues Fachvokabular erworben. Zu vielen Aufgaben gibt es einen **Vocabulary Assistant**, der wichtige Wörter und Redewendungen übersetzt. In bildgestützten Hörverständnis- und Sprechübungen werden die neuen Sprachmittel geübt und angewandt. **Useful Phrases**-Kästen geben Hinweise auf den richtigen Gebrauch englischer Rechtsterminologie, während **Did you know?**-Kästen sowohl fachliche als auch lexikalische Informationen zusammenfassen, die für den englischsprechenden Rechtsexperten nützlich sind.

Realitätsnahe Rollenspiele – mit ausgefeilten Rollenkarten in den **Partner files** im Anhang – ermöglichen, das Erlernte zusammenfassend einzuüben. Sie schaffen zudem Sprechanlässe in realistischen rechtlichen Situationen, in denen sich Lernende in ihrem beruflichen Alltag häufig wiederfinden. Im Abschnitt **Final Provisions** schließt jede Unit mit einem anspruchsvollen, authentischen Text aus der aktuellen Fachpresse, der zur persönlichen Stellungnahme auffordert und zu weiteren Diskussionen anregt.

Nach erfolgreichem Abschluss aller Units lässt sich mithilfe des Kreuzworträtsels in **Test yourself!** wichtiges Vokabular aus dem SHORT COURSE überprüfen.

Der Anhang enthält einen **Answer key** zur selbstständigen Kontrolle der Lösungen, **Partner files**, die **Audio-Transkripte**, eine zweisprachige **A–Z wordlist** sowie **Useful phrases and vocabulary**.

1 Forming a company

Preamble

Lawyers often have to use these terms when talking about company law. How many of them are you familiar with? Can you explain any of them?

articles of association / incorporation • freelancer • equity / company capital • tangible assets • commercial register • unlimited liability

For further help, look at the terms in the text below.

1 Anke Hermann, a lawyer, goes onto the Internet and finds the following information about different legal structures in Germany. Fill the gaps with the words supplied below.

CHAMBER OF COMMERCE

INFORMATION FOR INVESTORS AND ENTREPRENEURS FROM ABROAD

Legal structures in Germany

agreement • cash • debts • on your own • owners • personal • profits • publicly • separate • shareholding

Working for yourself

If you work for yourself, you are self-employed either as a sole trader or a freelancer. The technical term for your business is a sole proprietorship. You automatically become a sole trader when you register a trade with the trade office and manage the business ____________________[1]. However, German law regards some self-employed people e.g. journalists, architects, translators and teachers differently. These people are **freelancers**. They do not need to register with the trade office. A tax number from the local tax office is sufficient. As a self-employed person you have **unlimited liability** for your ____________________[2].

Partnerships

These business organizations do not have a separate legal identity from the people who form them. This means that the partners are liable for the debts of the firm with their ____________________ [3] assets. A partnership which is not registered with the **commercial register** is a GbR *(civil law partnership)*. A written partnership ____________________ [4] is recommended but it is not required by law. If a partnership is registered, it becomes, for example, an OHG *(ordinary partnership)*. Partners do not need to provide a minimum amount of **equity** by law but they can agree to pay capital into the firm if they wish. Moreover, they are not only ____________________ [5] but also directors of the company.

Limited companies

These business organizations must be registered with the commercial register and have a ____________________ [6] legal identity. This means the members are only liable for the size of their ____________________ [7] in the company. It is the company that is liable to creditors with its assets. In the case of a GmbH *(company with limited liability)* the minimum equity is EUR 25,000. However, this company capital does not have to consist entirely of ____________________ [8] – **tangible assets** e.g. machinery can also be contributed. The company must also have a written agreement – called the **articles of association**. An AG *(public limited company)* is often – but not always – a company whose shares are traded ____________________ [9] i.e. anyone is allowed to buy them. For these companies the minimum equity is larger and there are different requirements regarding the number of directors and accounting procedures.

A new "mini-*GmbH*" is planned. Its equity will be EUR 1 but the company will have to make use of some of its ____________________ [10] every year to build up equity of EUR 25,000 to become a full GmbH.

DID YOU KNOW?

The British and American English terms for companies often vary. These are just broad equivalents. Be sure you use the correct term in the appropriate jurisdiction *(Gerichtsstand)*.

Germany	UK	USA
Einzelunternehmen	sole proprietorship	sole proprietorship
GbR	civil law partnership / non-trading partnership	partnership constituted under civil law
OHG	ordinary partnership	general partnership
KG / GmbH & Co. KG	limited partnership (LLP)	limited partnership
GmbH	private limited company (Ltd.)	privately/closely held corporation
AG	public limited company (plc)	publicly traded corporation

In the USA, the abbreviations "Inc." and "Corp." are very common, but they do not indicate the public trading status of a company. In fact, they are the only abbreviations acceptable in all states for a company that has registered itself as a separate legal identity. An LLC (Limited Liability Corporation) is a different type of company, similar to but not the same as a private limited company. An LLC combines the tax flexibility of a partnership with the personal liability protection of a corporation.

2 Here are some points of view about different legal aspects of the company types presented above. What do you think?

2

3 Anke Hermann has a consultation with her client Matthew Osborne, a UK businessman, who owns and manages a company in Bremen called "Osborne Real Estate GmbH".

Part 1: Listen to part 1 and answer the following questions:

1 What is the nature of Matthew Osborne's business?

____

2 What plans does he have for the two directors in his company?

____

3 When did he form his limited company?

____

4 What area of business does he now want to move into?

____

5 Why does he want to reduce his involvement in the commercial property sector?

____

3

Part 2: Listen and complete Anke Hermann's written notes.

Osborne Real Estate GmbH would offer each owner a guaranteed minimum income that is lower than ____________________ a.

Osborne Real Estate GmbH would earn money in two ways:

1) administration charge of ____________ b or ____________ c cents per m²
per month,

2) performance bonus of ________________ d % of all income above
guaranteed annual minimum.

Where one or two apartments in a property are empty, minimum income for those owners is financed from ____________________________ e.

Where several apartments stand empty, minimum income has to be financed by ________________ f. Big risk! Client must ________________ g – otherwise his liability towards the owners could bankrupt his whole company.

Owners are functioning as a group, and sharing risks. So it won't be possible for client company to have a ____________________________ h.

VOCABULARY ASSISTANT

acquire *kaufen*
commercial property *Geschäftsimmobilien*
holiday apartments *Ferienapartments*
landlord *Vermieter*
objects (clause) *Gegenstand des Unternehmens*
owner *Eigentümer*
property (UK), real estate (US) *Immobilien*
rental income *Mieteinnahmen*
rent out (US), let (UK) *vermieten*
shareholder *Teilhaber*

4 In principle, Matthew Osborne has a potentially good idea, but there are a lot of issues to consider. Work in small groups.

- Should Osborne Real Estate GmbH finance the minimum rent from its own funds? Is there an alternative?
- Is it possible to guarantee the minimum rent for a limited period of time, e.g. only three months?
- What kind of legal structure would be the right one to make cross-subsidising rent possible?
- Is the whole idea too risky or too complicated?

Look at the list of issues. What should Matthew do and why? Use the following phrases:

I would (wouldn't) advise him to … .
I (don't) think he should … .
He (really) ought to … .
He could always … .

5 A day later Anke Hermann sends Matthew Osborne the following letter. Put the six paragraphs into the correct order.

Hermann und Dietz Rechtsanwälte
Am Wall 14 • 28195 Bremen • Tel. (0421) 6248210 • E-Mail: hd.rae@web.de

Matthew Osborne
Managing Director
Osborne Real Estate GmbH
Ostertorstraße 116a
28195 Bremen

17 March 2…

Dear Mr. Osborne

Holiday apartment lettings concept

a) However, there are two issues I would like to draw your attention to. Membership of the GbR would require each partner to be an owner/landlord of at least one apartment in the property, so Osborne Real Estate GmbH would not be allowed to be a member of this partnership. Of course, the partnership agreement would require all partners to accept your company as the managing agent for the GbR, with you as its representative. However, you would have no control over who the managing partner was.

b) If, on the basis of the points I have outlined above, you decide to form a GbR, the specific steps necessary would be as follows: first of all, we would need to discuss the precise nature of the business relationship between your company and the owner/landlords so that we can draft a partnership agreement. Then it would be your job to persuade prospective "buy to let" investors to sign up with the partnership. Following that, I would suggest depositing an appropriate sum as a guarantee – we can always recover this sum if the civil law partnership is not formed. Last of all, we would notify the tax office of the formation of the partnership and it would allocate the company a tax number.

c) Following our consultation yesterday I would like to set out your legal options as follows:

d) The second issue is the question of the minimum guaranteed rent. I strongly advise you to limit your liability here. I suggest drafting a clause to this effect in the partnership agreement and depositing an appropriate sum in a bank account as a guarantee. This sum – which we can talk about in more detail later - would effectively be the limit of your liability towards the partnership. Without this measure, the entire assets of your GmbH would be at risk.

e) If you would like to proceed with this matter or if you have any questions, please do not hesitate to contact me.

f) As you explained, the owners of the individual apartments in one property would be acting as a group and sharing risks as a group. Therefore, they would have to operate within a clear legal structure. I would suggest forming a GbR (a civil law partnership) for this purpose. This is a relatively uncomplicated legal structure which does not need to be entered in the commercial register. All of the specific details concerning the precise relationship between your company and this civil law partnership would be set out in the relevant partnership agreement. You would simply form a new civil law partnership for each separate property.

Yours sincerely

Anke Hermann

VOCABULARY ASSISTANT

guarantee *Bürgschaft*
managing partner *geschäftsführender Gesellschafter*
partnership agreement *Gesellschaftsvertrag*
prospective *potential, possible*

Answers: 1 ☐ 2 ☐ 3 ☐ 4 ☐ 5 ☐ 6 ☐

6 Discussion

1 How does this advice compare with yours?
2 Is there a way in which Osborne Real Estate could make itself the managing partner of the GbR?
3 Is it a problem if Osborne Real Estate is not a partner in the GbR?
4 Are there any further important issues that Anke Hermann has failed to mention?

DID YOU KNOW?

The word *Gesellschaftsvertrag* is not easily translated in English. In the UK, this would be **partnership agreement** or **deed of partnership** in the case of non-incorporated firms. In a private incorporated firm, there are two documents: a **memorandum of association**, which is publicly accessible and gives information about the location of the company, its owners, its objects etc. and **articles of association**, which are to do with the internal arrangements within the company. This second document is not publicly accessible.
In the US, the **articles of incorporation** is the document that has to be filed with the relevant state. This document is required of incorporated and non-incorporated firms alike.

7 In her letter Anke Hermann uses some verb + noun pairs, e.g. *to set out details, to form a company, to limit liability*. The following verb + noun pairs are common when getting started in business. Try to make pairs.

VERB	NOUN
1 register / run	a restrictions
2 raise / contribute	b debts / costs
3 submit / reject	c the commercial register
4 draw up	d business
5 impose	e capital
6 incur	f shares
7 view / inspect	g a company
8 obtain	h a certificate of incorporation
9 issue / hold	i an application (for entry in a register)
10 conduct	j a contract / a partnership agreement

8 Fill in the gaps using the verb + noun pairs above. You may have to modify the verb.

1 In the UK any member of the public is allowed to ______________ ______________ at Companies House to get information about a particular company.

2 A plc can extend its equity base by ______________ ______________.

3 Under normal circumstances a company should not commence trading until it has ______________ ______________.

4 A freelancer is only required to notify the tax office in order to be allowed to ______________ ______________.

5 The commercial register can ____________ ____________ for registration if the proposed name of the company is too similar to a name that already exists.

6 The law does not require partners in a civil law partnership to ____________ ____________, but most solicitors would recommend this.

7 When a private limited company tries to ____________ ____________, the bank often insists on securing any loan against the personal assets of the company's owners.

8 In a partnership the members bear personal liability for any ____________ which the partnership might ______________.

USEFUL PHRASES

Some expressions for giving advice and making recommendations require a gerund and some an infinitive.
Note: Some phrases are appropriate when spoken but are not appropriate in a formal written context.

Gerund (-ing)

I (would / wouldn't) *suggest* / *recommend* **doing** something to limit your liability.
How /What about **doing** something to limit your liability? **(spoken)**

Infinitive

I think / don't think you *should* **allow** yourself to be liable for unlimited sums.
I (strongly) *advise* you *to* **limit** your liability.
You *could* always **change** the objects clause. (**spoken**)
You *ought* to **change** the objects clause. (**spoken**)
Why don't you **change** the objects clause? (**spoken**)

NB. All the above phrases can be used when you are advising someone directly. If you are discussing what **he/she/they** should do, use the phrases listed in exercise 4.

If you would like to use *recommend* and *suggest* for a third party, the structure is as follows:

I recommend / suggest that s/he should + infinitive

9 Look at an extract from a letter to a client' s lawyer, whose partnership has got into difficulty.

Dear …

… I formed an accountancy partnership with David B. five years ago, specializing in accountancy services and tax advice for small businesses. My partner has now informed me he wishes to leave our firm in order to accept a partnership with a large firm specializing in accountancy for large corporations. My problem is that I do not think I can afford to buy him out right now. What is more, the new firm is not very far away. I mention this because our partnership agreement states that if a partner leaves, he should not do business within a 5-mile radius of his old firm. I am, of course, worried that David B. might take some of our existing clients with him to his new firm. …

Rebuild the lawyer's suggestions below:

A

1 You could always ...

2 I suggest ...

3 You really ought ...

4 I wouldn't advise you ...

5 I don't think you should ...

6 I don't recommend ...

B

a ... worry about the cost of buying your partner out yet. Your partnership agreement states that this payment would only be due at the end of the next financial year.

b ... ascertain the precise value of the firm. Then you will know how much it will cost to buy your partner out.

c ... trying to come to a binding agreement about existing clients. You will lose some clients, but don't want to lose too many.

d ... to terminate the existing partnership with immediate effect. David B. is not going to act in your firm's interests any more.

e ... bringing in a new partner straight away. Wait and see how much business you have before you rush into such an important decision.

f ... to invoke the 5-mile radius clause. It's probably not enforceable anyway.

Is there any advice you don't agree with? Do you have any other advice for the client?

VOCABULARY ASSISTANT

ascertain *feststellen, bestimmmen*
binding *verbindlich*
buy s.o. out *j.en auszahlen* due *fällig*
enforceable *durchsetzbar* with immediate effect *mit sofortiger Wirkung*

DID YOU KNOW?

Lawyer is a general term which we use to refer to someone who has learnt the law and has a licence to practise. In the US, lawyers are often called **attorneys** or **attorneys-at-law**. In England and Wales, the legal profession is not unified, so a distinction is drawn between **solicitors**, who have rights of audience in only some courts, and **barristers**, who specialize in advocacy (i.e. the art of presenting cases in court) and who have a right of audience in all courts. Generally, a solicitor will consult with his or her client and prepare a brief. This brief is then passed on to a barrister who will present the case in court. Successful and distinguished barristers are often invited to become a Queen's Counsellor. Such barristers always use *QC* after their name.

10 A client consults a lawyer about forming a company. Before you begin your consultations, agree the country of jurisdiction *(Gerichtsstand)* with your partner.

PARTNER FILES Partner A File 01, p. 70
Partner B File 01, p. 75

Use language for making recommendations and giving advice in your consultation. After you have finished the activity, tell the class what you agreed to do.

USEFUL PHRASES

It is often important to give reasons and explain things step by step.
Note: Words like **firstly** and **first of all** aren't used in the same way.

Enumerating reasons

Firstly, the company is investing with minimum risk ...
Secondly, the investor receives 75 % of any rent above the minimum.
Thirdly, ...
Finally, ...

Explaining the steps involved in a procedure

First of all, we need to discuss the business relationship between ...
Next, I would suggest depositing ...
Following that, it would be your job to persuade ....
Last of all, we would notify the tax office ...

NB. Be careful with **at first**. We use this to express the fact that we thought something initially and then changed our minds.

Example: At first it seemed a good idea to form a private limited company. Later we realized that this would be too expensive and too complicated.

11 Below are some extracts from a presentation about the new *mini-GmbH* in Germany. Fill in the gaps using words from the Useful Expressions box.

"____________ 1, I'd like to provide you with a bit of background on company types in this country and the rationale behind these different types. ____________ 2 I'd like to go on to look in more detail at the proposed *mini-GmbH* or – to give it its more formal name – *Unternehmergesellschaft*. ____________ 3, I'd like to look at the time scale which the law thinks will be appropriate for converting a *mini-GmbH* into a full *GmbH*. ____________ 4, I'd like to discuss with you some of the criticisms that have been expressed about this new type of company."

...

"I'd like to move on now to talk about the *mini-GmbH* in more detail. ____________ 5. I wasn't much in favour of the *mini-GmbH*. But, on reflection, I feel it has some distinct advantages. ____________ 6, it enables entrepreneurs to get into business quickly; ____________ 7, it is supposed to convert itself into a full *GmbH* at a later stage so the risk to creditors is relatively small and ____________ 8 it provides a much needed alternative to the English limited company."

12 The speaker says later in her presentation that she intends to discuss some criticisms which have been expressed about the mini-GmbH. What, in your view, might these criticisms be?

13 Here is a table from the website of the German Chamber of Commerce and Industry (DIHK) *(adapted)* which provides potential entrepreneurs and investors with information on German company types. Put the items of information in the box into the appropriate place in the table.

1	Shares cannot be traded publicly.	2	Accounting obligations are stricter than for GbR	3	Registration with trade office (possibly)	4	Partnership agreement is not required but is advisable.	5	Only the founder can manage the business
6	GbR (civil law partnership)	7	Normally two (one is possible)	8	Only with tax office	9	two	10	OHG (ordinary partnership)

Legal form of company	Sole proprietorship	(c)	(f)	Unternehmer-gesellschaft "mini-GmbH"	GmbH (limited liability company)
Mainly suitable for	small businesses and start-ups	freelance professions / non-trading organisations	medium-sized and large companies	start-ups	medium-sized and large companies
Advantages	no involvement of other people necessary	easy to form	greater freedom to manage business than in the case of a corporation	low minimum capital members not personally liable to third parties	members not personally liable to third parties
Minimum number of people	one	two	(g)	Normally two (one is possible)	(i)
Minimum capital	none	none	none	EUR 1	EUR 25,000
Formal costs	low	low	low	fairly low	fairly low
Formal documentation	little / none	none	partnership agreement	articles of association (certified by notary)	articles of association (certified by notary)
Formal registration requirements	(a)	(d)	commercial register	commercial register	commercial register
Liability	unlimited personal liability of the owner	unlimited personal liability of the partners	unlimited personal liability of the partners	liability of members towards company only to the level of the equity of the company	liability of members towards company only to the level of the equity of the company
Additional information	commercial register entry necessary where turnover and profits are large (b)	(e)	(h)	25 % of annual profits must be allocated to equity of company until it can be converted to a full GmbH	(j) minimum capital can consist partly of tangible assets

14 A lawyer gives a client information on forming a company. Work with a partner.

PARTNER FILES
Partner A File 02, p. 70
Partner B File 02, p. 75

Final Provisions

Read these readers' letters to the editor of the law supplement of *The Times* newspaper. What advice would you give them?

Letter 1

Dear Editor

Two years ago I set up a part-time Internet business with a friend (both of us work on other projects as well). Each of us invested a few thousand pounds on a web designer and hosting costs. We agreed that I would administer the site while he would look after the business and commercial side, (filing company accounts, sorting VAT, developing partnerships, etc).
At the beginning of the year, one of his other businesses started doing well so he abandoned our project leaving me with a backlog of work *(viel unerledigte Arbeit)* I could not manage alone, which led directly to the demise *(Kollaps)* of the business and the loss of my original investment.
Do I have any legal recourse *(Regressanspruch)*?

Yours faithfully
John Williams

Letter 2

Dear Editor

My business partner and I ran a financial advisory partnership until a few years ago when we converted it into a private limited company. We retired last year and the company ceased trading *(Geschäftsbetrieb einstellen)*.
We have now received a claim *(Schadensersatzanspruch)* relating to advice given a few years ago when the business was still a partnership. We have received advice that "it is not legally possible or binding for a firm to transfer liabilities without the consent of the claimant or creditor, and even then only in certain circumstances". What can we do?

Yours faithfully
Gordon Davies

Over to you

Now go to page 104 and read at the bottom the replies to these letters that were written by experts.

- Do you think the law is being fair to the two people who wrote the letters?
- Are there any differences between the legal position as explained in the two replies and the legal position in your own jurisdiction?

2 Employing people

These people are talking about different aspects of their contracts of employment. Work with a partner and make a list of the points they are sure or unsure about.

Preamble

Now look at your list again. What, in your experience, does a standard contract of employment usually say about these points? Discuss this with other members of the group.

DID YOU KNOW?

Contracts often start with a **preamble**. This is like an introduction. One of the preamble's functions is to state the parties in the contract. This means, for example, the main body of an employment contract doesn't mention the name of the company or the name of the employee; it simply refers to **"the Company"** or **"the Employee"** – usually written with a capital letter.

An employment contract contains information on salary or pay. The heading for this part of the contract or clause is usually called **Remuneration** (BE) or **Compensation** (AE).

A **severance** (BE) or **separability / severability** (AE) clause is very common. It ensures that the contract as a whole remains valid even if one or two clauses in it become invalid. The two parties are simply required to renegotiate the invalid clauses as quickly as possible.

1 Below are some clause headings taken from a standard contract of employment. Match them with the correct clauses. One heading does not fit anywhere.

Absence • ~~Applicable law~~ • Competition • Confidentiality • Duration of contract / Term of employment • Duties • Leave entitlement • Severance • Working hours

Clauses

1 ______________________

Business and in-house documents of all kinds, including records on official matters, may only be used for business purposes and must be stored with care. Such documents are to be **surrendered** to the management upon termination of employment.

2 ______________________

For the **duration** of this contract or until its termination and for the following two years, the Employee **undertakes** to, in no way, be employed by competitors of the Company or by a firm connected with them without the **consent** of the Company.

3 ______________________

The contract of employment **commences** on 1 April and shall run for an unlimited period of time.

4 ______________________

In the event of certificated illness or other hindrance through no fault of the Employee, the entitlement to salary continues to exist for a period of six weeks.

5 ______________________

The Employee is **entitled** to 30 working days' **leave** per year. The Employee must schedule the dates of this holiday so that the needs of the Company are taken into account.

6 ______________________

The Employee shall be in charge of developing spreadsheet software applications for corporate clients.

7 *Applicable law*

The construction, validity and performance of this contract shall be governed in all respects by English law.

8 ______________________

The invalidity of individual **provisions** does not affect the legal force of the contract as a whole. **In lieu of** the **inoperative** provisions, a provision shall be agreed upon which conforms as closely as possible to the stated commercial objectives of the parties.

2 Match the words or expressions highlighted in the contract on page 17 (column A) with words or expressions that have a similar meaning in simple English (column B).

A contract vocabulary	B simple English
1 surrender	a agreement
2 duration	b holiday
3 undertake	c have the right to
4 consent	d terms
5 commence	e promise
6 leave	f in place of
7 be entitled to	g length (of time)
8 provisions	h invalid
9 in lieu of	i give back
10 inoperative	j begin

4

3 Two days ago Cathy O'Brien from Dublin, Ireland was offered the position of software developer at Softline GmbH, a Cologne-based company. Today she has a meeting with the Head of Human Resources, Torsten Schwarz, to go over some of the details of her contract. Listen to the conversation and decide if the statements below are true or false.

VOCABULARY ASSISTANT

assume *annehmen, ausgehen von*
clarify *klären* draft *Entwurf*
entitlement *Anspruch*
flat-hunting *Wohnungssuche*
to that effect *diesbezüglich*
union rate of pay *Tariflohn*

1 According to Torsten Schwarz the normal working week isn't Monday to Friday. ☐
2 Cathy is prepared to work weekends now and then. ☐
3 Torsten states that it is unusual to carry over annual leave into the following year. ☐
4 Cathy might be prepared to accept extra pay in compensation for unused annual leave. ☐
5 In the company, ordinary employees get paid for overtime or they get the time back. ☐
6 As a senior member of staff, Cathy will not be entitled to receive any pay for overtime. ☐
7 Cathy wants something in her contract that entitles her to be paid for any overtime done if her line manager agrees. ☐
8 Torsten tells Cathy that it will be possible to change the overtime clause in the contract. ☐

DID YOU KNOW?

The words **clause**, **section** and **paragraph** can often be confusing. Contracts, agreements and articles of association consist of **clauses**. Each clause contains a provision. **Sections** are used to refer to state legislation. Both clauses and sections may consist of more than one **paragraph**. In such cases we would refer to clause 3, paragraph 2 or section 25, paragraph 3. However, contracts sometimes refer to clauses as sections!

USEFUL PHRASES

The following expressions are useful when referring to a legal document or explaining its content.

It says in clause 3 **that** ...
The termination clause clearly **states** / **stipulates that** ...

According to clause 5 the employee must ...
It says here ... **This simply means that** ...

4 Work with a partner to discuss some problems relating to a contract of employment.

PARTNER FILES
Partner A File 03, p. 70
Partner B File 03, p. 75

5 Torsten speaks English very well, but has difficulty finding the right tone in letters and e-mails. He would like to write his e-mail in a friendly but formal style. Fill the gaps with the words below.

resolve • got back • you see • sort out • talk about • just • here are • wish • getting in touch with • discuss • sorry • pretty • contacting • I am attaching • unfortunately • please • returned • want • I apologise • reasonably

Delete Reply Reply All Forward Print

From: t.schwarz@softline.de
To: cathy.obrien@hotmail.com
Subject: amendments to contract

Dear Mrs. O'Brien

Regarding our meeting last week, ____________[1] for not ____________[2] you earlier. ____________[3], our solicitor was in court in Frankfurt for most of last week and only ____________[4] yesterday.

As we agreed, ____________[5] the amendments to your contract as suggested by him. I think you'll find that overall they ____________[6] the issues you raised with me last week ____________[7] well.

Could you have a look at them and let me know me by the end of the week at the latest if there are any points you still ____________[8] to ____________[9]? I can then try to have the contract ready for signing by the middle of next week.

In the meantime, if there are any other matters where I can be of help, ____________[10] give me a call.

I look forward to hearing from you soon.

Best regards
Torsten Schwarz

6 Read the attachment Torsten Schwarz sent and discuss with a partner the two questions below.

Suggested amendments to Cathy O'Brien's contract of employment

Please note: the suggested amendments to the contract have been added in italics.

1.2 Duties and Working Hours
The normal working time shall be 38 hours per week. *This will also include weekend work from time to time. For provisions regarding overtime, see 4.5.*

6.2 Leave Entitlement
… The Employee is also entitled to compensation for up to 15 days of unused holiday based on the amount of her basic salary as defined in 4.1. *Up to and no more than seven days of unused holiday may be carried over into the following financial year provided these days are taken before 1st March and insofar as the taking of these days is not detrimental to the interests of the Company.*

4.5 Remuneration
There is no entitlement to *financial* compensation for overtime, Sunday or holiday work or other extra work. *Any overtime worked may be taken as time in lieu provided that the taking of such time is consistent with the interests of the Company and has the express agreement of the Employee's line manager.*

1 On what point(s) has Cathy got what she wanted?
2 On what point(s) has she got less than she wanted?

VOCABULARY ASSISTANT
consistent with *übereinstimmend mit*
detrimental to *abträglich*
express *ausdrücklich*
line manager *direkte(r) Vorgesetzte(r)*
provided *vorausgesetzt, dass* provision *Bestimmung*

7 Cathy replies to Torsten's e-mail. First sort the words into sentences and then put the sentences in the correct order.

From: cathy.obrien@hotmail.com
To: t.schwarz@softline.de
Subject: amendments to contract of employment

Dear Mr. Schwarz

☐ a compromise / I / a / suggest / Perhaps / could / here

____

☐ b to / happy / suggested amendments / with / I / clauses 1.2 and 4.5 / the / am

____

☐ c let / if / know / be / possible / Please / might / me / this

____

☐ d take / extra month / to / give / it / would / which / an / It / me / also / in

____

☐ e year / would / stands / still / eight days' leave / I / As / risk / up to / a / it / losing

____

____

☐ f the / sending / amendments / Thank you / yesterday / me / for / contract

____

☐ g by / would / the end of / any / leave / have to / February / I / Furthermore / take / unused

____

____

☐ h by / end / ten days / taken / the / you / to / Would / to / March / agree / be / of ?

____

____

☐ i me / 25 / minimum / days' / would / a / of / This / leave / guarantee

____

☐ j am / about / leave entitlement / little / However / clause / a / the / I / concerned

____

Kind regards
Cathy O'Brien

8 **Cathy reaches an agreement on her leave entitlement clause. Now, however, she must resign from her current job. Look at her letter and at the two clauses below which she refers to. Has she resigned in accordance with her contract?**

41 Ratra Road
Dublin 7

Mr. John Flannagan
Human Resources Manager
Intelligent Solutions Ltd.
28 Parnell Place
Dublin 1

15th November 2…

Dear John

In accordance with clauses 7.2 and 7.5 of my contract of employment I hereby serve notice of my wish to resign from my current position as Software Development Co-ordinator with effect from 1st January of next year. I will be taking up a new position in software development with a leading developer of telecommunications software in Germany.

I would like to take this opportunity to thank you for your friendly and professional support during my time at this company.

Best regards

Cathy O'Brien

Cathy O'Brien

Extract from Cathy's contract

7.2 A probationary period of six months has been agreed. During this time employment can be terminated with two weeks' notice. Thereafter, a notice period of three months to the last day of the month is in effect.

7.5 Notice of termination must be delivered in writing. The Employee must address her written notice to the Personnel Director.

USEFUL PHRASES

Contracts often talk about **rights** and **obligations**.

Rights
The employee **is entitled** / **is allowed** to / **has the right to** / **can** take 30 days' leave.

Obligations
The employee **must** / **is required to** / **is obliged to** / **has a duty to** / **has to** treat all company data and files with complete confidentiality.

9 **Look at the following clauses from Cathy's contract. Match the sentence halves below. Decide which sentences are talking about rights and which about obligations.**

Extract from Cathy's contract

3.2 For the life of this contract or until its termination and for the following two years, the Employee agrees to in no way be employed by competitors of the Company or by a firm connected with them.

3.4 If the Company does not expressly waive the ban on competition in writing upon termination of this contract, it shall pay to the Employee compensation in the amount of 50% of her average fixed annual salary (see 4.1) for the last three years per year for the life of the ban on competition. The compensation shall be paid in monthly instalments at the end of each month.

7.6 Upon termination of the contract the Employee may be released from work for the length of the notice period. The Employee's entitlement to full pay remains unaffected.

1 According to 3.2 the Company can ...
2 According to 3.4 the Company, but not the Employee, can ...
3 If the Company makes this decision, it is required to ...
4 If the Company decides to enforce 3.2, the Employee is entitled to ...
5 7.6 states that the Company is entitled to ...
6 If the Employee is sent home, the Company has to ...

a ... receive half pay for a period of two years.
b ... send the Employee home on the day she hands in her notice.
c ... pay her full salary for the rest of her period of notice.
d ... communicate this to the Employee in writing.
e ... restrict the Employee from working for a competitor for two years after leaving the Company.
f ... decide not to make use of clause 3.2.

VOCABULARY ASSISTANT

instalment *Rate*
release *freistellen*
unaffected *unberührt*
waive *verzichten auf*

10 John Flannagan, Head of Human Resources at Intelligent Solutions Ltd., is unhappy about Cathy's plans and so he consults Mary Wilson, a solicitor specialising in employment law. During the meeting they make reference to the clauses above.

5

Listen to the conversation. Which of the three statements below best sums up what is said?

1 John and Mary want to stop Cathy going to work for Softline, the mobile phone company.
2 John and Mary want to send Cathy home today.
3 John and Mary are, to different degrees, worried about confidentiality.

Listen again and choose the best option or options to complete the sentences below:

1 Mary says that the company ...
- a ... can prevent Cathy from starting on 1st of January if it wants to.
- b ... can't really prevent Cathy from starting on 1st of January.
- c ... intends to prevent Cathy from starting on 1st of January.

2 John isn't happy about Cathy moving to Softline GmbH ...
- a ... because it is poaching the company's staff.
- b ... because confidential information might change hands.
- c ... because Softline is an important co-operation partner.

3 To invoke the competition clause would mean that the company ...
- a ... could employ Cathy on half-pay for the next two years.
- b ... could prevent Cathy from working for Softline GmbH for two years.
- c ... would have to prove that Cathy had contact with a competitor.

4 In the end, there is a risk that ...
- a ... the company won't be able to prove its case in court.
- b ... that the company's response will be more dramatic than is really necessary.
- c ... that Softline GmbH will reduce its level of involvement with Intelligent Solutions Ltd.

VOCABULARY ASSISTANT

gardening leave *Freistellung von der Arbeit bei vollem Gehalt*
invoke a clause *sich auf eine Klausel berufen*
poach staff *Personal abwerben*

We don't hear the end of the meeting. What would you suggest if you were the in-house lawyer?

11 You and your partner are solicitors, one from Intelligent Solutions Ltd. and the other from Softline GmbH. Work with your partner to discuss Cathy's contract.

PARTNER FILES
Partner A File 04, p. 71
Partner B File 04, p. 76

After you have finished, present the outcome of your negotiation to the rest of the group.

USEFUL PHRASES

We agreed / decided to ...
The best option here is to ...
In return they will ...
By way of compensation they will ...

Final Provisions

Read the article from *The Times* Newspaper about dress codes.

Tie case throws dress codes into confusion

The collar and tie faces an uncertain future in the office. Willie Manners and Juliet McMyn look at the implications of a recent tribunal ruling.

Last week's ruling that a man who worked in a JobCentre was a victim of sex discrimination because he was made to wear a collar and tie has been hailed (*begrüßen*) variously as a "victory for common sense" and the death knell (*Totenglocke*) of the traditional white-collar male dress code.

Matthew Thompson, an employee in a JobCentre at Stockport, objected to (*Einwände haben*) the "smart casual" dress code imposed by the Department for Work and Pensions because it required men to wear a collar and tie but made no similar clothing requirements for women. The code, which banned employees from wearing fleeces without management consent, was at first assumed to be a joke. But when Thompson was disciplined for refusing to wear a tie, it all became less amusing.

Thompson's real bugbear (*etw sehr Irritierendes*) was that dress standards did not apply equally between the sexes. While men had to wear a tie, women were allowed to wear T-shirts or even football shirts to work without fear of reprisal (*Diziplinarmaßnahmen*). Thompson claimed that the males were victims of "gender stereotyping" and that the dress code was discriminatory. The tribunal agreed. But its ruling, which may go to appeal (*in Revision gehen*), is surprising. It appears to be in direct contrast to the previous view that an employer could impose different dress codes on the sexes as long as the rules were enforced equally; it certainly paves the way for other employees who dislike formal dress to bring similar claims. We may, for instance, hear from Dennis Fitzpatrick of Birmingham, another JobCentre employee, who was banned from wearing jeans to work. He recently reported for duty in a kilt, lumberjack shirt and a loud multicoloured tie. Of his employers, he said: "They seemed happy for me to go to work like this, even though I looked like a pillock (slang: a stupid person)."

At the hearing on Thompson's case, the panel was invited by his employer to consider the meaning of the term "smart casual" and, in particular, what kind of clothing would be considered acceptable in an office. For men, smart trousers with a collar and tie were suggested. For women, skirts, dresses, trousers and fitted or loose tops. From such analysis it is clear that while society's ideas of acceptable apparel (*Kleidung*) for a man have remained fairly constant, its views on dress codes for women have changed radically. (*abridged*)

Willie Manners and Juliet McMyn – Macfarlanes law firm

Over to you

- Do you agree with Matthew Thompson and Dennis Fitzpatrick?
- Do you have any sympathy for the employer, in both cases the local JobCentre?
- Is there a dress code at your place of work?
- Does it apply to different groups of people equally? How do you feel about it?

3 Buying and selling goods and services

Preamble

Here are some sales managers having a consultation about contracts with the in-house lawyer. How would you answer their questions?

1 Look at the preamble to a contract for the supply of goods and find the following information:

1 What is the product?
2 Which party manufactures the product?
3 Where is there detailed information about the product?
4 Who plans to buy the product?

CONTRACT OF SALE

Preamble

This agreement is made this 1st day of March 2… by and between Digital View plc, with its principal place of business at 17, Hopkinson Way, Andover, SP10, ENGLAND, (hereinafter "PURCHASER") and Pixeltechnik GmbH, with its principal place of business at Paderborner Straße, 63, 30539 Hannover, GERMANY, (hereinafter "SELLER") and its permitted sub-contractors and assignees.

Whereas:

- PURCHASER, a manufacturer of electrical goods, wishes to purchase the goods (hereinafter "GOODS") specified in Annex 1 hereto and subject to the terms and conditions of this agreement:
- SELLER, a manufacturer of high-performance LCD screens, wishes to manufacture and supply the aforementioned GOODS.

Whereby it is agreed as follows:

USEFUL PHRASES

Compound adverbs

In a preamble to a contract – this part of a contract is also called "recitals" – the words **whereas** and **whereby** can seem confusing. In general, **whereas** in this context simply introduces the information about the transaction that the two parties want to enter into and **whereby** introduces the main part of the contract in which all the agreed clauses are set out.

The difference between ***hereafter*** and ***hereinafter*** is as follows: ***hereafter*** means "from this point in time" and ***hereinafter*** – "from this point in the document". Equally, ***thereafter*** means "from that point in time".

In "The supplier ***hereby*** agrees that …." the word "***hereby***" means "as a result of this document". In "The obligations ***hereunder*** of the supplier cannot be assigned except with …", the word "***hereunder***" means "under this agreement".

Moreover, words like ***hereto***, ***thereof*** and ***herewith*** are not as difficult as they look.

Here is used in a legal document to refer to this document.
There is used to refer to documents or agreements other than this document itself.

Depending on the context, a preposition can be added to ***here*** or ***there***.
For example: "The parties to this agreement" can become "The parties ***hereto***".
"The whole sum or any part ***of*** it" can become "The whole sum or any part ***thereof***".

Adjective + preposition

Contracts often contain difficult adjective + preposition word pairs, like ***subject to***, ***pursuant to*** or ***conditional upon***. Basically, all three mean the same as ***in accordance with***.

2 Fill in the gaps using one of the compound adverbs below.

hereto • hereby • hereinafter • thereafter • therein • therewith • thereof • thereunder

1 This agreement shall become effective on the date of signature. Any changes in the manufacturing process (see 4.5.1 above) undertaken ________________ by the SUPPLIER must be notified to the COMPANY without delay.

2 If delivery of an entire order or of any part ________________ is subject to delay, the following provisions shall apply:

3 XYZ plc (____________________ the LICENSEE) shall distribute the aforementioned GOODS.

4 Prices and product numbers are set out in Appendix IV ____________________ .

5 The project plans (Appendix II) and the specific start and finish dates set out ________________ shall be of the essence.

6 This Agreement replaces the existing agreement between the parties. However, the SUPPLIER's obligations ________________ in respect of warranties shall remain until the expiry of all relevant warranty periods.

7 The PURCHASER ________________ agrees to place an order each calendar month for the duration of the agreement for the following quantities:

8 The SUPPLIER is, without exception, bound by the aforementioned quarterly delivery schedule. Failure by the SUPPLIER to comply ________________ shall entitle the PURCHASER to the following penalty payments:

3 Here are some clauses from the contract between Digital View plc and Pixeltechnik GmbH. Put the sentence parts below back into the contract on page 29, where you see the boxes.

1 for a period of three years after delivery
2 are free from the rights of third parties
3 subject to the provisions for termination in 8.1 and 8.2 below
4 the number of items specified in Annex 2
5 any defective goods at no additional cost to PURCHASER
6 PURCHASER shall be entitled to terminate the agreement by giving 21 days' written notice to SELLER
7 shall be Hampshire County Court, Southampton, England
8 PURCHASER may reduce the agreed price for the order by 2 %

1 Delivery

1.4 Failure on the part of SELLER to meet the terms of delivery shall entitle PURCHASER to invoke the following penalty clause terms: for every week or part thereof by which the delivery date is exceeded, [ ] [a]. The rights of PURCHASER under 8.1 shall remain unaffected.

3 Minimum Orders

3.1 PURCHASER undertakes to purchase during the first 24 months following signature of this agreement [ ] [b]. The minimum amount ordered each calendar month shall be according to the details set out therein.

4 Price

4.1 The price charged for the goods shall be in accordance with the price list set out in Annex 2. The stated price shall be binding on both the seller and the purchaser for the duration of this agreement.

5 Duration

5.1 This agreement shall be for a period of two years from the date of signature [ ] [c].

5.2 The agreement shall be renewed automatically for a further period of one calendar year unless either SELLER or PURCHASER terminates in accordance with the provisions contained in 8.2 below.

8 Termination

8.1 Should SELLER: (i) fail to provide satisfactory performance of this agreement or (ii) fail to fulfil any of its obligations hereunder or (iii) become bankrupt or have a winding up petition made against it or have a liquidator or administrator appointed, [ ] [d].

8.2 In all other cases, notice to terminate must be made in writing by either SELLER or PURCHASER no later than 90 days in advance of the expiry date as defined in 5.1 above.

10 Warranties

10.1 SELLER warrants that the goods will comply with the specifications as set out in Annex 1 and will be free of defects (other than those caused by incorrect usage or operation by PURCHASER) [ ] [e].

10.2 Pursuant to the above warranty SELLER guarantees that after receipt of written notice from PURCHASER it will promptly repair or replace at PURCHASER's option and to PURCHASER's entire satisfaction [ ] [f].

11 Warranty of title

11.1 SELLER warrants that the GOODS [ ] [g] SELLER shall indemnify PURCHASER on demand against any claims made by third parties in this regard.

12 Applicable law and jurisdiction

12.1 This agreement shall be governed by the laws of England and Wales.

12.2 Exclusive place of jurisdiction for all disputes arising out of or in connection with this agreement [ ] [h].

DID YOU KNOW?

Warranty has two meanings in contract law.

1 It can be the statement that a manufacturer makes to the purchaser in which the repair or replacement of defective goods within a certain period of time is guaranteed.
2 It is the word used for a **term** in a contract that is not a condition. A **condition** is an essential element of a contract. If it is breached, then the other party has the right to terminate the whole contract. A **warranty** is not an essential part of a contract. If a **warranty** is breached, the contract as a whole remains in force for both parties.

Expiry date is the end of a period for which something is valid. It is often called **expiration date** in American English (AE).

The heading **"Duration"** in a contract can also be **"Term"**, especially in AE. This use of the word **"term"** has nothing to do with the meaning of term above. Here it means a period of time.

Force majeure is sometimes referred to as **"act of God"**. This clause covers all of the things that can happen which might make performance impossible, but over which the parties have no control e.g. storms, natural disasters, unannounced strike action.

4 Read the dictionary definitions below and choose the correct term among the words underlined in the contract on page 29, which fit the definition.

1 ________________ person appointed by the court to manage the affairs of a bankrupt company

2 ________________ to be in accordance with

3 ________________ conditions (in an agreement)

4 ________________ to make use of or apply a clause in a contract

5 ________________ formal request to have a company closed down

6 ________________ a guarantee issued to the purchaser of an article promising repair or replacement in case of defects

7 ________________ to hold a person safe or secure against a risk

8 ________________ to go beyond a set limit (quantity or time)

9 ________________ imposing an obligation which one must fulfil

10 ________________ to state or describe something in writing

6

5 You are the in-house lawyers at Digital View plc. At a meeting with the purchasing department you are asked the following questions about the agreement with Pixeltechnik GmbH. Listen to each question and note your answers below. Then share your views with the class.

1 ______________________

2 ______________________

3 ______________________

4 ______________________

5 ______________________

6 ______________________

7 ______________________

8 ______________________

USEFUL PHRASES

Legal English often uses **past participles** to make sentences more compact. Instead of:
"The price which is charged for the goods shall be ..." or "... the number of items which is specified in Annex 2"
The contract says:
"The price **charged** for the goods shall be ..." or
"... the number of items **specified** in Annex 2"

Present participles are also used to make sentences more compact. So instead of:
"The agreement which exists between the parties is due to expire at the end of this year."

We can say:
"The agreement **existing** between the parties is due to expire at the end of this year."

6 Put the verbs into the sentences below. Decide if you want a *present participle* or a *past participle*. Be careful! There are two verbs which you don't need.

arise • claim • dispatch • entitle • fail • find • impose • lead • list • reach

1 Any goods ______________ to be defective must be replaced within 48 hours to the full satisfaction of the purchaser.

2 Any decision ______________ by the arbitrator is binding on both parties.

3 The prices ______________ in Annex 1 fail to take account of possible quantity discounts.

4 The purchaser is indemnified against any loss or injury to a third party ______________ out of any product defect as defined in 6.4 above.

5 The 1,000 euro charge ______________ on the supplier by my client is completely in accordance with the penalty clause in the agreement.

6 A transport strike ______________ to delays in delivery is only covered by the *force majeure* clause to a limited extent.

7 Any products ______________ to meet the agreed specifications will be returned to the supplier at the supplier's expense.

8 The compensation ______________ by the purchaser is, in our view, unreasonable.

7 The contract runs well for 15 months. Then Pixeltechnik GmbH is forced to send the following letter to Digital View plc. Read the letter and answer the following questions:

What is the problem?
How quickly can Pixeltechnik solve the problem?

Pixeltechnik GmbH
Paderborner Straße 63
30539 Hannover
Tel: +49 511 648 31 50
E-mail: pixel.technik@t-mobile.de

23rd September 2…

Mr. Gary Thorne
Head of Purchasing Department
Digital View plc
17 Hopkinson Way
Portway Industrial Estate
Andover
SP10
England

Dear Mr. Thorne

Recall of all batches from TZ64/0 to TZ64/9

I regret to inform you that we have to recall the above ten batches of LCD screens for use in digital cameras. Unfortunately, it has come to our attention that a chemical processing error has caused minor inconsistencies in the candlepower of the screens. They failed to pass all of our quality controls and must therefore be regarded as defective.

I appreciate that, in recalling a total of 5,000 screens, I am causing considerable inconvenience to your company. I apologise for this and will endeavour to dispatch to you 1,000 screens within the next ten days and the remaining 4,000 within 21 days at the latest.

Please accept once again my sincere apologies for this error. If you have any questions or would like to discuss this matter further, do not hesitate to contact me.

Yours sincerely

Johannes Hörner

Johannes Hörner
Managing Director

What is your overall opinion of the letter? Is the tone appropriate? Is the information sufficient? Give some examples.

8 You are a lawyer in the legal department of Digital View. Decide how your company should respond to this problem. Consider the following options and give reasons for your choices:

- accept Pixeltechnik's apology
- accept the apology but take steps to obtain compensation or to impose penalties
- suggest another alternative

9 Now listen to a consultation between Herr Hörner, Managing Director of Pixeltechnik GmbH, and Mr. Evans, an English contract lawyer, working for an international law firm in Germany.

7

Part 1: The problem

Are the following statements true or false?

1 Digital View replied to Pixeltechnik's original letter of 23rd September. ☐
2 The Production Manager first realized there was a problem when he noticed a chemical processing error. ☐
3 Herr Hörner is sure that the screens still conformed to the product specifications agreed in the contract. ☐
4 The technicians only carried out tests on the product once every ten days. ☐
5 Some defective LCD screens had already been delivered to Digital View. ☐

8

Part 2: The dispute

Answer the following questions.

1 Name three reasons why Herr Hörner thought he had avoided a dispute with Digital View.

____

____

____

2 What does Digital View now intend to do?

____

____

3 On what legal grounds is it trying to do this?

____

4 Why is it important to Pixeltechnik that the contract runs at least two years?

____

____

10 You are solicitors advising Herr Hörner. Discuss the following questions with a partner.

1 To what extent are the following points significant?
   a In his letter of 23rd September, Herr Hörner described the 5,000 LCD screens as "defective".
   b Pixeltechnik already seemed to have reached a compromise with Digital View.

2 To what extent can it be argued that Digital View is not justified in invoking 8.1 (i)?
3 How important is the concept of "reasonableness" here?
4 If Digital View wants to terminate the contract, what are its rights and obligations?
5 Is the absence of a dispute resolution clause significant?

Now decide what advice to give your client.

11 Contracts and legal correspondence often contain words with negative prefixes e.g. *in*valid, *in*solvent. Look at the list of adjectives below and match them with the correct negative prefix.

IR • UN • IN • IM • DIS

1 ____	valid	8 ____	foreseeable
2 ____	lawful	9 ____	partial
3 ____	enforceable	10 ____	confirmed
4 ____	satisfied	11 ____	correct
5 ____	reconcilable	12 ____	complete
6 ____	affected	13 ____	reasonable
7 ____	effective	14 ____	satisfactory

USEFUL PHRASES

The words "**valid**", "**enforceable**" and "**effective**" sometimes cause confusion.

A work permit or residence permit can be **valid**, i.e. it has the correct stamps on it or hasn't expired. A contract of employment can be **effective**, i.e. it is in use and has legal relevance. As an employee, I might have certain rights or claims with respect to an employer that are **enforceable**, i.e. I can go to court and the court will ensure that my rights are respected or my claims met.

A contract that has no legal basis – because, for example, one of the contracting parties acted under duress or because the object of the clause is unlawful – is **void**.

12 Practise some vocabulary with a partner.

PARTNER FILES
Partner A File 05, p. 71
Partner B File 05, p. 76

USEFUL PHRASES

Lawyers need to get information from their clients and summarize what the client has said, to direct the consultation and to express their own point of view. The following questions and expressions can be useful.

Getting information
Could I start by asking you when / why / how the problem began?
And what happened then?
What did you do then?
How did the other party react to this?
Could you explain why ...?

Getting the client to refocus
Let me take you back to ... .

Checking and clarifying
Are you suggesting that ...?
So, if I understand you correctly ...
Could you explain what you mean by ...?

Expressing an opinion
As I see it ...
Our best option would be to ...

13 A client and a lawyer discuss contract issues. What advice did your lawyer give you?

VOCABULARY ASSISTANT

comply with *einhalten, erfüllen*
invoice *Rechnung*
offer *Angebot*
prospective buyer *potentieller Käufer* reject *ablehnen*
tiles *Dachziegel* valued at €10,000 *mit einem geschätzten Wert von €10,000*

PARTNER FILES
Partner A File 06, p. 72
Partner B File 06, p. 76

14 Fill in the gaps with words from the unit. There are two words which you don't need!

binding • bound • comply • defective • expire • invoke • specifications • terminate • terms • warranty

1 Any ________________ items must be replaced within five working days to the full satisfaction of the purchaser.

2 The insolvency of the supplier entitles the purchaser to ________________ this agreement with immediate effect.

3 The prices hereby agreed shall be ________________ on both parties for a period of 24 months.

4 The goods must be manufactured according to the ________________ set out in Annex 2.

5 The ________________ of delivery state that the supplier remains liable for the goods until they have been unloaded at the specified delivery point and signed for by the purchaser.

6 Your failure to ________________ with this completion date entitles my client to impose the following financial penalties:

7 To ________________ the termination clause because some of the goods delivered were not of the required standard would be seen as unreasonable.

8 The agreement will ________________ exactly twelve months following its date of signature.

Final Provisions

Read the article about a famous case in contract law.

Flour power and contract law

By Franklin G. Snyder

Legal scholars from around the world are celebrating a momentous *(sehr wichtig)* event: a broken steam engine shaft at a flour mill in Gloucester. That shaft gave rise to *(verursachen)* the most widely known case in the history of common law: the 1854 decision of Hadley v Baxendale.

Great cases sometimes have trivial causes. In an era engrossed by *(sehr beschäftigt mit)* news of impending *(drohend)* war with Russia, few cared about that broken shaft. Two people who did were Joseph and Jonah Hadley, the mill owners. They needed that shaft and as it could be repaired only in Greenwich, they hired Pickfords, the removal company, to take it from Gloucester by the next day. For some unexplained reason, the shaft took several days to arrive. During the delay, the mill lay idle *(unbenutzt)*.

The Hadleys sued for the delay. The question before the court was whether Pickfords was liable for *(haften für)* the money that the Hadleys had lost while the mill was without its shaft. The court's answer was no. Since Pickfords did not necessarily know that the mill would be idle until the shaft could be returned – there might have been a spare *(Ersatz)* – the court found that the company could not be charged with those damages. Its opinion announced what came to be known as the "foreseeability" test for contract breaches: you cannot be held liable for losses that you could not reasonably have anticipated *(voraussehen)*.

How did this rather mundane *(gewöhnlich)* dispute become a fixed star in the legal firmament *(Himmel)*? There are two reasons. The first was the growth of contract law. Before the 19th century, many commercial relationships were regulated by custom *(Gebrauch)*, not by individual agreements. There was, in fact, no body of law called "contracts". Secondly, the world of 1854, like that of today, was one of revolutions in transport, communications, economics, politics and society. It was the first era of "globalisation".

An era of rapid change needs contract rules that are predictable, but also flexible. And Hadley is the embodiment *(Verkörperung)* of the common law's success at dealing with change. Its "foreseeability" rule encourages people to engage in transactions by protecting them from damages that could not be anticipated. But by avoiding a fixed rule – say, that the carrier is never liable for such lost profits – it allows for flexibility when things change. Next time, the carrier might be aware that there is only one shaft and that it had better *(wäre gut beraten)* take precautions or charge *(mehr Geld in Rechnung stellen)* more in exchange for the greater exposure *(Verlustrisiko)*.

The Hadleys' old mill is, coincidentally, being restored. For me, a law professor who studied Hadley 20 years ago as a student, it is fitting that the mill is being adapted to face a new century, just as Hadley's rule has allowed us to adapt to futures about which we could only guess.

(abridged)

Over to you

- How does the law deal with the concept of foreseeability in your jurisdiction?
- Do you share the author's enthusiasm for this case as an example of clarity and flexibility?
- What, in your opinion, works better in contract law? Case law (the Anglo-Saxon tradition) or codified law (the tradition in continental Europe)?

4 Protecting intellectual property

Preamble

How, if at all, can the law give protection to the following and prevent copying?

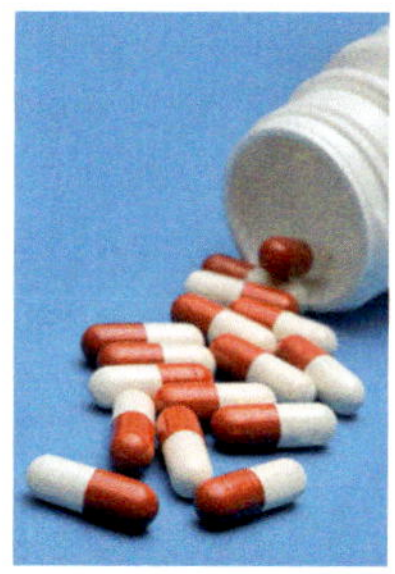

- a new drug substance
- a 19th century violin concerto
- a new perfume
- a scientific theory, e.g. e = mc2
- a distinctive chocolate product
- a new TV news show format
- a new novel
- a sauce or drink with an unmistakeable flavour
- a toaster that downloads the weather forecast and toasts the day's temperature onto your bread.
- a photo of St. Stephen's cathedral in Vienna at sundown

DID YOU KNOW?

Copyright is an exclusive right granted to someone who creates a literary, artistic, musical or other creative work. It is the right of the author or composer to reproduce or sell this work. The right can be granted to others e.g. publishers or record companies. Oddly, the period of **protection** (in the EU) depends on the type of work under copyright. In the case of a novel, for example, it is the author's lifetime plus 70 years; in the case of a song it is 50 years from the date when the song was first released or broadcast.

A **patent** gives an inventor the exclusive right to exploit an invention for a period of 20 years. The date when this period begins (**priority date**) is not when the invention comes onto the market as a finished product but when the patent application is made. If the **patentee's** rights are **infringed**, the remedies available are to seek a court **injunction** and to sue the infringing party for **damages**.

A **trade mark** is a design, logo or wording which distinctively identifies a product. When a trade mark has been **registered** the owner has the exclusive right to use this trade mark in connection with the products listed in the original registration. If a competitor starts to use a trade mark that is so similar to this registered trade mark that **confusion** might arise in the mind of the public, this offence is called **passing off**. As long as a trade mark is used, it lasts for ever.

Original shapes or patterns or designs can be protected using a **design right**. The period of protection here is 25 years.

1 Work with a partner. Put the words back into the following three texts. Then try to guess how the court decided in each case and why.

competitor • copyright • damages • format • general • infringement • patented • plaintiff • trade mark • validity

a

A TV show compère, Mr. Green, developed a show ______________[1] whereby ordinary members of the public would be given the chance to perform to a nationwide TV audience. The TV public then send in a postcard to vote for the best act and this act was carried over into the following week's show. The TV show was a huge success in the UK. A short time later a similar show was launched on TV in a different country by the Broadcasting Corporation of New Zealand. Mr. Green claimed ______________[2] for infringement of his intellectual property rights but the defendant argued that a talent show is of such a ______________[3] nature that it cannot be afforded ______________[4] protection.

Green v Broadcasting Corporation of New Zealand (1989) RPC 700, Privy Council

b

Mölnlycke AB ______________[5] a refastenable disposable nappy. The Velcro-like fastener enabled parents to make a quick check of the baby's nappy without complication. Procter & Gamble, a ______________[6], went ahead and began to manufacture very similar nappies whereupon Mölnlycke claimed ______________[7] of its patent. The defendant questioned the ______________[8] of the patent on the grounds of obviousness.

Mölnlycke AB v Procter & Gamble Ltd (No 5) (1994) RPC 49, Court of Appeal

c

The ______________[9] owned a restaurant in London called WAGAMAMA. The name is a Japanese word meaning "healthy eating and healthy living" and the restaurant was a Japanese-style noodle eatery. The defendant opened an Indian restaurant with the name RAJAMAMA. This word doesn't mean anything. When the plaintiff first brought an action against the defendant for ______________[10] infringement and passing off, the latter responded by changing his restaurant's name to RAJA MAMA'S. The plaintiff was still not satisfied so the case came to court.

Wagamama Ltd. V City Centre Restaurants plc (1995) FSR 713, Chancery Division

2 Now have a look at the answer key to see what was decided in each case.

- Do you agree with the court's ruling in each case?
- Would a court decide in the same way in your jurisdiction? Why or why not?

3 The following agreement was reached a few years ago between a film production company and a publisher regarding the film rights for a novel.

This Agreement is made this day, 1 May 2...

between: Index Films Inc.
34 West 62 Street.
New York 10023
USA

(hereinafter PURCHASER)

and: Blackbird Ltd
218 The Strand
London WC2R 1AT
England

(hereinafter OWNER)

Whereas:

a) OWNER, a publishing house, is the ***only*** / ______________[1] and exclusive owner of all rights, including copyrights, to the original literary work entitled "BLACKOUT" by **Adam Parks** (hereinafter WORK).

b) PURCHASER ***wants*** / ______________[2] to produce or cause to be produced a motion picture based upon or adapted from the WORK.

c) PURCHASER has ***bought*** / ______________[3] from OWNER and OWNER has ***given*** / ______________[4] to PURCHASER an exclusive option to purchase the worldwide motion picture rights (hereinafter RIGHTS) to the WORK under the terms and conditions hereinafter ***written down*** / ______________[5]

2 OWNER ***guarantees*** / ______________[6] that it has the exclusive right and authority to enter into and to fully perform this agreement and to grant exclusively to PURCHASER the rights herein.

3.1 The exclusivity period for which PURCHASER has acquired RIGHTS shall ***begin*** / ______________[7] either a) on the date this Agreement is signed by both parties and shall end exactly ten years later to the day or b) upon the initial release of the motion picture as defined in Appendix A and end exactly eight years later to the day, whichever period ***ends*** / ______________[8] first.

4.1 The purchase price of $... is payable on the date this Agreement is signed by both parties.

5.2 Should a third party wish to produce or cause to be produced a motion picture based upon or adapted from the WORK within the exclusivity period as defined above in this Agreement, this will only be ***possible*** / ______________[9] with the express written ***agreement*** / ______________[10] of both PURCHASER and OWNER.

Are the following statements about the agreement true or false?

☐ 1 The copyright to "Blackout" by Adam Parks will be sold to the purchaser.
☐ 2 Index Films can commission another film production company to make the planned film.
☐ 3 This agreement is not restricted in any way to certain geographical regions.
☐ 4 The exclusivity period is for eight years.
☐ 5 If Index Films makes the film and then another film maker wants to do a remake before this agreement has expired, this will not be possible.

4 **The words in *italics* in the contract on page 39 are in simple English. Replace them with the standard legal vocabulary below.**

acquired • commence • consent • desires • expires • granted • permissible • set forth • sole • warrants

DID YOU KNOW?

Quite often contracts contain sentences that begin with "should". These are not requests or questions but "if" sentences. We can rewrite clause 5.2 without changing the meaning as follows:

"If a third party wishes to produce ..., this will only be permissible with the express written consent of ..."

5 **Some years later, Fabian Stein, the head of Linke Hand Produktion, a Berlin-based film production company, is interested in doing a remake of the film version of *Blackout*. Read the following letter from their solicitors in London and, using the agreement between Index Films and Blackbird for reference, write a *number* or *date* in each of the six gaps.**

Walker & Field Solicitors • 52 Gloucester Road • London SW7 4QT

Herr Fabian Stein
Linke Hand Produktion
Am Comeniusplatz 4
10243 Berlin
Germany

1st May 2...

Dear Mr. Stein

Acquisition of motion picture rights to "Blackout"

With regard to your plans to acquire the motion picture rights to the novel "Blackout" by Adam Parks, I am forwarding you the written response I have now received from the attorneys for Index Films in New York and from Blackbird, the publishers of the work. In addition, I enclose an abridged copy of the original agreement between these two parties.

The legal situation is relatively straightforward and I am confident that we will be able to negotiate a satisfactory agreement. However, I would like to draw your attention to the following points.

As you can see from the preamble of the original agreement, it was signed on ________________ [1] exactly four years ago. Index Films actually released their motion picture one year after signing the agreement. As a result, in accordance with clause ________________ [2], the exclusive worldwide motion picture licence will expire ________________ [3] years after the release date. Since we are not negotiating a new agreement but simply asking Index Films to waive its right to exclusivity, we too will be bound by the same expiry date. In other words, you would have no more than ________________ [4] years in which to produce your film. Moreover, after the expiry date, any other party would be free to negotiate exclusive film rights with the publisher. Of course, your right to exploit the film you produce will exist in perpetuity.

The publishers have implicated their willingness to consider your acquisition of the motion picture rights within the defined exclusive period in return for financial consideration. With your permission, I would be happy to draw up a Letter of Intent – to be signed by yourself and the publishers. The final compensation figure would not be fixed at this stage.

However, clause ________________ [5] makes clear that the consent of both the original parties is necessary, so we must also reach an agreement with Index Films. Clearly, Index Films will be looking for financial compensation in return for waiving their exclusivity rights. Nevertheless, it should be borne in mind that their film was released ________________ [6] years ago and is generating hardly any income now. In my view, Index Films will not wish to drive too hard a bargain here, so it should be possible to reach an agreement for no more than EUR 100,000. With your permission, I could draw up a draft agreement and set up a video conference to negotiate with the attorneys in New York.

I would be grateful if you could let me know how you would like me to proceed in this matter. If you have any questions concerning the above, please do not hesitate to contact me.

Yours sincerely

William Field

William Field

Enc. Abridged copy of original agreement between Index Films and Blackbird
Written reply (22nd April 2…) from Blackbird, publishers
Written reply (28th April 2…) from Mason and Gonzales, attorneys-at-law, New York

VOCABULARY ASSISTANT

abridged *gekürzt* attorney (AE) *Rechtsanwalt* bear in mind *consider* bound by *gebunden an* consideration (legal) *Gegenleistung* draft agreement *Vertragsentwurf* drive a hard bargain *hart verhandeln* generate income *Einnahmen erzielen* in perpetuity *auf ewig* in the region of (IRO) *von ungefähr + Zahl* letter of intent *Absichtserklärung* release (film) *herausgeben* waive *verzichten auf*

6 William Field often uses a linking word or phrase to join a sentence with the previous sentence. What words or phrases does he use to do the following?

express a contrast	____________________
provide additional information	____________________
express a consequence	____________________
state an opinion	*In my view*
restate or reformulate some information	____________________

7 Use linking words and phrases from exercise 6 to complete these sentences.

We can apply for a court injunction against any further use of the logo. ____________________[1], we should consider suing the infringing party for damages.

This product clearly has a commercial application. ____________________[2], it may be difficult to demonstrate that it is really innovative.

The songwriter in question sold the copyright to the record label. ____________________[3], she cannot prevent the record label using this song in a commercial for a product of which she disapproves.

The film studio is prepared to waive its right to exclusivity. ____________________[4], it will allow another filmmaker to make a film of the same book.

The court accepted that a quiz show is not normally capable of copyright protection. ____________________[5], it ruled in this case that certain features of the show format were so distinctive that a right to protection existed.

9

8 Index Films and Linke Hand Produktion hold a video conference. Listen and decide if the statements below are true or false.

1. Fabian Stein is not willing to pay royalties. ☐
2. According to Fabian Stein, Index Films would not be allowed to keep the proposed down payment of €20,000 if the film flopped. ☐
3. Jake Glover changes his mind about a success-related payment. ☐
4. Fiona Martinez makes it clear that her client has plans to negotiate with a third party. ☐
5. If Linke Hand Produktion can't get the agreement of the publishers within three months, it won't have to make a down payment. ☐

VOCABULARY ASSISTANT

cease *aufhören* clarify *klären*
conditional upon *abhängig von*
down payment *Anzahlung* drag on *sich hinausziehen*
proposed *vorgeschlagen* rejection *Ablehnung* royalties *Tantiemen*
secure *erhalten, bekommen* viable *realisierbar* zilch (AE slang) *nichts*

9 Read the draft agreement below. Now listen again and fill in the gaps.

MOTION PICTURE RIGHTS AGREEMENT

This Agreement is made this day, 15 May 2… between Linke Hand Produktion with its registered business address at Am Comeniusplatz 4, 10243 Berlin, Germany (hereinafter ______________[1]) and Index Films Inc. with its registered business address at 34 W. 62nd Street, New York, 10023, USA (hereinafter ______________[2]).

Whereby it is agreed as follows:

RIGHTS HOLDER, a film production company, wishes to surrender its right of exclusivity in respect of the motion picture rights as defined in Annex 1.

RIGHTS HOLDER shall surrender its right of exclusivity in respect of the above mentioned motion picture rights to PURCHASER. As consideration PURCHASER, on condition that it acquires permission from Blackbird, (hereinafter ______________[3]) to film a re-make, shall pay a total of EUR______________[4]. An initial sum of EUR______________[5] shall be payable to RIGHTS HOLDER upon the acquisition of said rights following the signing of this agreement. Failure to make the initial payment within a period of ______________[6] following the signing of this agreement shall render said agreement null and void. No later than ______________[7] following the release of the movie by PURCHASER, a second and final payment of EUR______________[8] shall be payable to RIGHTS HOLDER.

USEFUL PHRASES

In a negotiation, **confrontational** language ("We can't possibly accept that.") states absolutes and closes down options. **Tentative** language ("We would find that difficult to accept.") makes the speaker's position clear, but leaves options open. Look at some examples from the negotiation you have just listened to.

Tentative		**Confrontational**
I'm afraid my board *might* find that figure a little low.		My board *will* find that figure too low.
We *might be able* to agree to …. if we could participate in …	is better than	We will agree to …. if we *can* participate in …
Any other type of agreement is*n't* really *workable* …		Any other type of agreement is *unworkable* …
€30,000 *isn't really* high *enough.*		€30,000 is *too low.*
I think €45,000 *is a little high.*		€45,000 is *too much.*

10 Use the information in the Useful Phrases box to make the statements less confrontational.

1 The payment period you suggest is too short.

____

2 Our share of the royalties is too low.

____

3 That's completely impractical.

____

4 If you extend the licence area to include Japan, we will accept royalties of 4%.

____

5 Our board will never agree to that.

____

11 Read the following extracts from a songwriting agreement and choose the best option to complete each of the statements below. Sometimes more than one option is possible.

An Agreement made this first day of March 2… between Global Music Inc. (hereinafter PUBLISHER) of the one part and Billy Ratt (hereinafter COMPOSER) of the other part.

1. COMPOSER agrees to compose and write music and lyrics for and during the period of this Agreement for and on behalf of PUBLISHER and hereby undertakes to assign, transfer and deliver to PUBLISHER or its successors the whole of the copyright to such music and lyrics and also to such music and lyrics written heretofore by COMPOSER for all countries of the world insofar as such copyright is not held by third parties.
2. COMPOSER makes the following productivity commitment: he will endeavour to deliver a minimum of ten compositions, each of which comprising three minutes of music on average, every year for the duration of this Agreement.

4. The rights of PUBLISHER include the right to make translations of song texts in foreign languages in consultation with COMPOSER. PUBLISHER is also entitled to grant licences or to authorise others to exercise rights hereunder in whole or in part and to assign in whole or in part the compositions hereunder. However, PUBLISHER shall not be entitled to assign the whole burden of this agreement without the prior consent of COMPOSER.
5. The term of the Agreement shall be for a period of three years from the date hereof. PUBLISHER shall have the option to renew this Agreement for a further period of three years.

8. PUBLISHER agrees to pay fees and royalties in respect of the compositions acquired hereunder to COMPOSER as follows:
   i) 12.5% of net receipts of PUBLISHER from sales of reproductions to public (CDs and vinyl).
   ii) PUBLISHER shall divide performing fees and broadcast fees between PUBLISHER and COMPOSER in the ratio 20% and 80% respectively, subject to any allocation for orchestral arrangements in accordance with the rules of the Performing Rights Society currently in force.
   iii) 12.5% of net receipts including the licensing of compositions for use in films, television programmes and commercials.

> 10. The royalty and free statements shall be made up to June 30th and December 31st in each year and shall include all receipts by PUBLISHER in that period. Such statements will be sent to COMPOSER within 28 days of the relevant date and be accompanied by a remittance for the amounts which are shown by the statement to be due and payable.

1 The composer is transferring copyright to the publisher ...
   a for all works composed during the lifetime of the agreement.
   b for all works which the composer has already composed, where the copyright is available.
   c but not to a third party which might acquire the rights of the publisher.

2 The publisher needs the composer's prior written consent ...
   a to make written translations of song texts.
   b to assign selected compositions to third parties.
   c to assign the entire agreement to a third party.

3 The agreement is drawn up so as to be able to run ...
   a for three years only.
   b for six years.
   c for more than three but less than six years.

4 When the composer performs his music in a concert, he will ...
   a receive 20% of the performing fees.
   b get possibly less than 80% of the performing fees.
   c collect more than 80% of the performing fees.

5 The performer will be paid his fees and royalties ...
   a twice a year.
   b whenever he likes.
   c no later than 28 days after the publisher has received them.

12 Two lawyers, each representing their client, meet to negotiate an exclusive copyright agreement.

PARTNER FILES
Partner A File 07, p. 72
Partner B File 07, p. 77

After you have finished the role-play, tell the class what amendments you agreed to make.

USEFUL PHRASES

Prefixes and suffixes are added to modify words.

Prefixes e.g. *in-*, *un-*, *over-*, *ex-*, are used to change the meaning of a word.
Suffixes e.g. *-ate*, *-able*, *-tion*, *-ship*, *-ment*, *-ism*, *-ee*, *-ity*, *-ly* are used to change both the meaning and the grammar of a word, i.e. to turn it into a noun, an adjective, an adverb.

Look at the following examples:
valid (adj.) – **in**valid (adj.), valid**ity** (n.), valid**ate** (v.)
patent (n. or v.) – patent**ee** (n. *person*), patent**ed** (adj.), patent**able** (adj.)
compose (v.) – compose**r** (n. *person*), compos**ition** (n.)
respond (v.) – respon**se** (n.), respond**ent** (n. *person*), respon**sive** (adj.), **un**respon**sive** (adj.)

13 Modify the words on the right so that they make sense in the following article.

J. K. Rowling determined to block RDR Books' Harry Potter 'rip-off'

by Dalya Alberge, Arts Correspondent, *The Times*

J. K. Rowling may be no stranger to battles against evil wizards and magical beasts but in her latest tussle she is preparing to appear in person in the American courts. The notoriously shy author is ready to testify herself to
protect her ________________[1] of Harry Potter against *own*
RDR Books, an independent American ________________[2], *publish*
next month. A US court is to decide whether she can block the publication of
an ________________[3] encyclopaedia of the wizarding world that she created. *authorise*
Rowling and Warner Bros., the Hollywood studio behind the epic film
________________[4] of the Hogwarts adventures, are taking legal action to stop *adapt*
RDR from profiting from a Harry Potter Lexicon, a 400-page guide to the Potter books and movies.

Accusing the book of lifting 2,034 of its 2,437 entries straight from her work, Rowling condemned the Lexicon as "a Harry Potter 'rip-off' ... [that] interferes with my rights as
a creator and copyright ________________[5]". She noted that RDR's attempt "to co-opt *hold*
my work for ________________[6] gain" was out of keeping with the spirit of the Potter *finance*
stories, which are "full of moral choices and ethical dilemmas". She claims that the
RDR book is not only an ________________[7] of her copyright but undermines her own *infringe*
planned lexicon. As she will donate its royalties to charity, "the ________________[8] *lose*
in such a situation would be the charities that I hope, eventually, to benefit".

David S. Hammer, co-counsel for RDR Books, said: "The Harry Potter Lexicon draws
material and ______________[9] from the Harry Potter series but is an entirely new piece *inspire,*
of work. It is a companion to Rowling's work, not a substitute for it".

In Britain and the US the work's ______________[10] holds the copyright; this prevents *create*
substantial passages being reproduced without ______________[11]. In Britain the "fair *permit*
dealing" provision allows use of copyright work for ______________[12] and review. In the *criticize*
US rule, the third party must make a contribution in reproducing material.

How do you think the court decided?

Final Provisions

Read the following article about IP rights and Internet Service Providers (ISP).

Why businesses should be wary of going after eBay fakes

by Gill Grassie specialist lawyer in intellectual property and information technology

The Internet may not be completely lawless, but it does facilitate *(fördern)* infringement of intellectual property laws on an unprecedented *(nie dagewesen)* scale.

How do you stop infringement when it is occurring on such a huge scale? Some companies have gone after the intermediaries such as eBay and Facebook, which provide the platform on which users can exchange goods and content so freely.

As the law stands, however, the middle men are generally immune from prosecution provided they remove infringing material from their sites as soon as they are notified of any potential infringement.

This sound like a sensible approach. It gives IP owners a quick and efficient mechanism for protecting their rights without placing burdensome *(lästig)* restrictions on popular sites such as eBay. But there is a catch *(Nachteil)*. IP owners keen to prevent copycatting *(Kopieren)* of their products, brands and ideas are often unaware that asserting *(fordern)* what they consider to be genuine rights may give rise to liability.

It may seem surprising, but IP owners who request intermediaries remove “infringing” products from their sites can themselves be sued *(verklagen)* for an injunction *(gerichtliche Verfügung)* and damages by the person or company they have accused.

The rationale *(Hintergründe)* is: an accusation that a business has infringed IP rights may result in that business ceasing *(aufhören)* to sell the allegedly *(angeblich)* infringing item. The business as a result may lose revenue, while public allegations may damage its reputation. The allegations may be made by a competitor or in bad faith *(in bösem Glauben)*; and even if they are made honestly, they may have no legal basis. In the UK, the law on patents, trade marks and designs makes such allegations actionable *(verklagbar)*.

Take eBay’s Verified Rights Owner (VeRO) programme. Under VeRO, you can notify eBay, via an online form, that there is material on the auction site infringing your intellectual property rights, such as a design right or a patent. eBay’s standard response is to remove the highlighted material without – understandably, for reasons of expediency *(Zweckmäßigkeit)* – any investigation of the merits *(sachlicher Gehalt)* of the claim. This immediately deprives *(entziehen)* the seller of his point of sale. eBay is contractually entitled to do this, but what if the VeRO notification is unfounded and there is no infringement? The alleged registered design right or patent may not have been granted. You may not actually own the right in question. Or there may just be no infringement.

Notification programmes such as VeRO are therefore a double-edged sword *(eine zweischneidige Sache)*: at first sight, they are useful tools for IP owners to have infringing material removed from the Internet. But unsuspecting IP owners can find themselves on the receiving end of an injunction or damages claim.

This puts the UK out of line with other countries in Europe and elsewhere, where no such provisions apply. For the time being, IP owners should be cautious about notifying an ISP of alleged infringement. *(adapted)*

Over to you

- In your opinion, is the procedure described a good approach?
- What remedies are available in your country to IP owners who are faced with ISP infringements?
- Do they risk being sued in the same way as their UK counterparts?

5 Mergers and acquisitions

Preamble

Read the "Quotations of the Week" from a US magazine.

- Who do you think the speakers might be?
- Which of them seem to be in favour of more regulation to control M & A?
- Which of them aren't? Where do you stand on this question?

Quotations of the Week

1 "When the company I work for was taken over, the price offered was far too high. The scope for savings through synergies was then overstated to justify the high price. The shareholders won, the directors won, all the legal and financial advisers walked away with their fees – and the price was paid by the employees. Within one year 2,000 jobs had been cut."

2 "The legal instruments in place for identifying and combating insider dealing are more than sufficient. Any more legislation in this area would simply restrict the freedom of companies to expand and would make them unattractive to investors."

3 "Naturally, we take the Federal Trade Commission (FTC) or its equivalent in other countries very seriously when we make an acquisition. But, to be quite honest, it has never intervened once. The whole thing is more of a formality, really."

4 "Mergers and acquisitions are a perfectly acceptable way for the market to optimise its efficiency. We were delighted when a large multinational wanted to acquire our small private limited company. The price was fair, no one lost their job and there was much more R & D money available to drive forward our most innovative ideas."

1 Read the article and fill the gaps using the words below. Two of the words don't fit anywhere!

acquired • expansion • merger • offer • results • takeover • targeted • uneven

Esskultur brings in CEO from US

The German company, *Esskultur AG*, which was formed two years ago out of the ________________[1] between the Swiss restaurant chain *Essen bei Fröbel* and the German cafeteria and snack bar chain *Kaffeekultur*, has responded to criticism

of its recent performance by its major shareholders. Following the disappointing ________________[2] posted by the sandwich bar chain *The Bread Company*, which was recently ________________[3] from a British hotel group for €60 million, and the failed ________________[4] bid which had ________________[5] the well-known restaurant chain *Pasta & Meer*, *Esskultur's* share price had fallen by 20%. The long-serving CEO Dr. Hans Kroll has agreed to make way for a fresh face – Matt Delaney, who has switched from his post as CEO of the major US fast-food restaurant chain *Lucky's*. Mr. Delaney is expected to sharpen up the company's performance and to put it back on an ________________[6] course. News of the appointment was received positively by the market, with *Esskultur's* share price rising by 6%.

10

2 Matt Delaney leaves the following voicemail message for Regina Möller, the recently appointed in-house lawyer. Listen and decide if the statements below are true or false.

1 Matt finds mergers and acquisitions confusing. ☐
2 There is documentation on mergers but not on acquisitions. ☐
3 Regina Möller has to explain to Matt where the hidden difficulties are. ☐

3 Regina mails the following document to Matt. The first and last steps are in the correct order. Put the remaining steps in the correct order.

Acquisitions – 10 steps

The following ten steps represent a standard procedure for carrying out mergers and acquisitions, starting with identifying a target company and finishing with the signing of a final contract with that company.

[1] An *initial screening* process is carried out to identify a target company.

[ ] (a) The board of management of the target company is approached. If the approach is not *rejected*, there will be a *mutual* exchange of information between the companies, but only after a *non-disclosure agreement* (NDA) has been signed by all persons involved at this stage.

[ ] (b) Based on the *outcome* of the due diligence process, the kind of transaction that is under consideration can be structured and the process of negotiation started.

[ ] (c) Assuming that *exploratory talks* have been successful, a *Letter of Intent* (LOI) is then drawn up and signed by the legal representatives of both companies. In our case, according to clause 15.1 of the company's *articles of association*, the CEO has this *power of representation*. Under German law the LOI is not legally binding in all respects.

[ ] (d) The process of due diligence can now be carried out. Anyone now entering the group of persons with insider information must be added to the list held by the *compliance* officer.

[ ] (e) At this late stage we may still not be *in the public domain*. Once a contract of sale is ready for signing, an Extraordinary General Meeting (EGM) would normally be held and the shareholders' *approval obtained*. According to clause 16.2 of the company's articles of association a simple majority of the registered share capital would be necessary.

[ ] (f) A potential target for takeover is selected. According to clause 14.2 of our company's articles of association, supervisory board approval must be obtained before the target company can be approached.

[ ] (g) In the gastronomy sector the due diligence process has to particularly include an assessment of public law compliance (i.e. health and safety, public building law etc. and food hygiene and labelling norms).

[ ] (h) From this point on our "Wertpapierhandelsgesetz", which is broadly equivalent to the US Securities Exchange Act, requires that the company's insider list – designed to prevent insider dealing - should be regularly updated to include anyone in the company with knowledge of the planned acquisition. This list must then be kept with the company compliance officer. *Failure to comply is a criminal offence*. The list can be required for inspection at any time by the "BaFin" – the German Federal Financial Supervisory Authority, which is *comparable to* the US Securities and Exchange Commission (SEC).

[10] We have now entered the public domain. The contract can be signed. Strictly as a formality, the acquisition should be reported to the "Wettbewerbsbehörde" – the competition authorities – *broadly* similar to the US Federal Trade Commission. In our case, our market share is not large enough in any of the sectors in which we operate for this to be a problem.

VOCABULARY ASSISTANT

approval *Zustimmung* articles (of the company) *Gesellschaftsvertrag* broadly *im weitesten Sinne* comparable to *vergleichbar mit* compliance *Vertragstreue* criminal offence *kriminelles Vergehen* exploratory talks *Sondierungsgespräche* failure to comply *eine Nichtbeachtung* initial *Anfangs-, Ausgangs-* Letter of Intent (LOI) / Memorandum of Understanding (US) (MoU) *geschäftliche Verpflichtungserklärung* mutual *gegenseitig* non-disclosure agreement (NDA) *Geheimhaltungsvereinbarung* obtain *erhalten* outcome *Ergebnis* power of representation *Vertretungsmacht* public domain *öffentlich* reject *ablehnen* screen *überprüfen*

DID YOU KNOW?

In M & A, reference is often made to certain laws or authorities. The following are broadly equivalent.

Germany	US	UK
Aktiengesetz	Corporation Law	Companies Act
Wertpapierhandelsgesetz	Securities Exchange Act	Securities Trading Act
BaFin	Securities and Exchange Commission (SEC)	Financial Services Authority (FSA)
Kartellamt	Federal Trade Commission (FTC)	Office of Fair Trading (OFT)

4 Through no fault of her own Regina has been using an older version of the articles of association of Esskultur AG. Have a look at the relevant clauses of the recently updated version and decide what information Regina needs to change or add.

14.2 The management board may, notwithstanding other instances provided for by statute, only carry out the following measures with the approval of the supervisory board:

(i) Formation, dissolution, acquisition or sale of participations in enterprises insofar as the obligation of the company exceeds in each individual case EUR 2 million.

15.1 The company is statutorily represented by two members of the management board or by one member together with an authorised signatory.

16.2 Resolutions are passed with a simple majority of the represented registered share capital unless a 75% majority or higher is necessary pursuant to statutory provisions or these articles. For resolutions requiring a 75% majority, see 14.2(i), (ii) and (iv) of these articles.

VOCABULARY ASSISTANT

authorised signatory *Unterschriftsberechtigte(r)* dissolution *Auflösung* enterprise *Unternehmen* equity *Aktienkapital* exceed *übersteigen* instance *hier: Fall* notwithstanding *unbeschadet* participation *hier: Beteiligung* pursuant to *gemäß*

5 Discuss the following questions.

1 What kind of things would an NDA contain? How effective are these agreements in practice?
2 What use do LOIs have if they are not fully binding under the law?
3 What might the SEC be looking for if it inspected the insider knowledge list?
4 Bodies like the Federal Trade Commission are very important. But is there a role for some monopolies in our society?

USEFUL PHRASES

Regina informs Matt of the US equivalent of various German laws or authorities.
Here are some useful phrases.

The German "BaFin"	is *(broadly, basically)*	equivalent to similar to comparable to like the same as	the US Securities and Exchange Commission.
	is *(a little, very, completely)*	unlike different from	
	differs *(slightly, completely)*	from	

6 What, in your view, are the similarities and differences between the following pairs? Some information has been provided. Use the phrases above.

Germany
- the *GmbH & Co. KG*
- the Unternehmergesellschaft (mini-*GmbH*)
- the *Rechtsanwalt*

UK
- the limited liability partnership
- the limited company (Ltd)
- the solicitor in England

- tariffs for German lawyers in civil claims
- the *Bürgerliches Gesetzbuch*
- the executive board *(Vorstand)* and the supervisory board *(Aufsichtsr at)*

US
- fees for US attorneys in civil claims
- civil law
- board of directors (BOD)

Example: "The *Bürgerliches Gesetzbuch* **is similar to** civil law in the US. However, in Germany civil law is set out in a civil code whereas in the US it consists of various acts of legislation but is based more on case law."

7 Each circle contains a noun surrounded by eight verbs. Six of these verbs make verb + noun pairs; two verbs don't. Cross these two out! Two verbs in each circle mean the same thing. Name them!

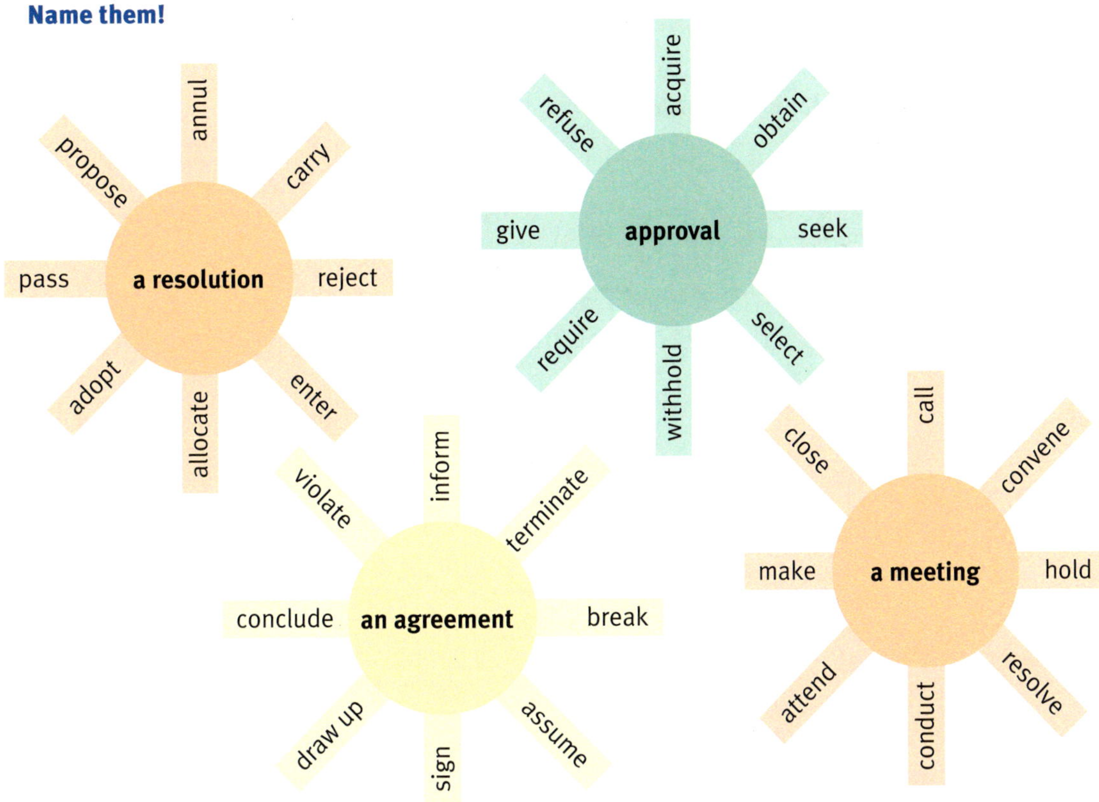

8 Use the pairs above to complete the gaps in the sentences below.

1 The management and supervisory boards were confident of the shareholders' support on the new share issue so they were unpleasantly surprised when the EGM voted to ________________ the ________________.

2 According to the company's articles of association the management board must ________________ the ________________ of the supervisory board before starting takeover talks with a company.

3 In view of the company's current difficulties, the board has decided to ________________ an extraordinary shareholders' ________________ to discuss the question of raising fresh capital.

4 The details of this takeover are so complex that it will take at least two weeks for the acquiring company's lawyers to ________________ an ________________.

5 If a shareholder cannot ________________ a ________________ in person, he can send a proxy to vote on his behalf.

6 At the AGM the shareholders voted to ________________ their ________________ of the actions of the board until full details of the terms of the acquisition deal were made available.

11

9 Six months have passed and Esskultur AG has identified a candidate for acquisition. Listen to the discussion between Matt Delaney (CEO), Regina Möller (in-house lawyer) and Oliver Stein (Finance Director) and answer the questions below.

PART 1

a Complete the fact file about the target company.

Fact file

Name of company: ____________________

Founded in: ____________________

Type of company: ____________________

No. of shareholders: ____________________

Country of registration: ____________________

Paid-up capital: ____________________

Current debts: ____________________

Current no. of cafés: ____________________

Style of cafés: ____________________

b Why is Oliver concerned about the leases for the different cafés?

c What do they decide to do about this?

12

PART 2

Answer the following questions.

a How would Oliver like to pay the current owners of *No Frills*, the target company?

b What would the legal status of *No Frills* be after the takeover?

c What agreement must be reached with the existing shareholders of *Esskultur AG* before the company can issue new shares?

d Why do both Oliver and Regina see a bank loan as an unattractive option?

e Does *Esskultur AG* have to consult its shareholders if it pays for *No Frills* out of its capital reserve?

f Why is the *Bread Company* mentioned in this discussion?

VOCABULARY ASSISTANT

capital reserves *Kapitalreserven* charge *Belastung* clearance certificate *Genehmigung* debts *Schulden* deplete *vermindern* drain (on finances) *finanzielle Belastung* findings *Ergebnisse* founder *Gründer* growth prospects *Wachstumschancen* in the region of (IRO) *ungefähr* newly issued shares *neu emittierte Aktien* operating costs *Betriebskosten* release of capital *Kapitalfreisetzung* share issue *Emission* sound *solide* upset *irritieren* venture capital *Risikokapital* waive a right *auf ein Recht verzichten*

Discussion

If *Esskultur AG* decides to finance the acquisition by issuing new shares, it will need the support of its shareholders.

- Why might existing shareholders be unhappy about waiving their right to buy newly issued shares?
- What arguments might Regina use to persuade them to support this plan?
- What do you think *Esskultur AG* should do to finance the acquisition? Are there any options they haven't considered yet?

10 During the meeting, Matt, Oliver and Regina use certain phrases to guide the flow of discussion. Stefan, the trainee lawyer, would like to manage meetings well but can't always find the right thing to say. Match each thought bubble with the correct expression.

a What do you mean by "leverage financing"?
b Could I just come in there?
c In principle, that's true but .... . I'm sure you're right but ... .
d Any views on that?
e I can't go along with that, I'm afraid.
f I'm sorry but I'm not quite with you there.
g I think Robert has a point here.
h I think we're getting away from the point here.

USEFUL PHRASES

A lot of colourful expressions are used in the context of takeovers. Here are a few common ones.

white knight	A friendly bidder who is brought in by the target company to outbid a hostile bidder.
black knight	This is a hostile bidder.
poison pill	A strategy adopted by the target company to make itself unattractive to the bidding company. It might involve a shareholders' rights plan, changes to voting and non-voting stock, or an acquisition which burdens the target company with higher levels of debt.
killer bees	These are the experts (lawyers, accountants etc.) employed by a target company to fend off a hostile takeover bid.
whitemail	This is the opposite of blackmail. Here the target company sells stock to a friendly third party at a discount price.
bear hug	The bidder offers a share price too high to refuse.
crown jewels	All the valuable assets of the target company.

11 Look at these clauses from a Letter of Intent.

4 Exclusivity

(1) Beginning with the signing of this Letter of Intent until six months after the end of the due diligence period, the Seller shall not hold any discussions, either directly or indirectly, with any third party about the *transfer* of the Shares or of the Company's business operations. The Seller shall end any current discussions.

(2) The exclusivity ends *in any event* upon the signature of the share purchase agreement or if one of the parties breaks off from the Transaction pursuant to clause 7(1).

(3) *In the event* the Seller breaches the exclusivity, it shall pay a *contractual penalty* in the amount of EUR 100,000 to the Purchaser. Further *claims* made by the Purchaser shall remain *unaffected*. The contractual penalty shall not be payable, if binding contracts are *concluded* between the parties.

7 Binding Effect

(1) This Letter of Intent does not create any obligation to carry out the Transaction. Both parties shall be entitled to break off the Transaction at any time before the share purchase agreement is signed, without having to provide any reason. The *notification* of breaking-off must be in writing.

(2) The break-off shall not affect the *applicability* of the *provisions* in 4(3) and 7(3) of this Letter of Intent; these provisions shall remain binding.

(3) If the Seller breaks off the Transaction, it shall pay a *lump-sum amount* of EUR 100,000 to the Purchaser as compensation for any expenses *incurred* in connection with the Transaction, unless the break-off is due to a breach by the Purchaser of the *confidentiality* obligation. If the Purchaser breaks off the Transaction, it shall pay a lump-sum amount of EUR 50,000 to the Seller as compensation for its necessary expenses, unless the break-off is due to of a breach by the Seller of the exclusivity or confidentiality obligations. Claims resulting from the breaking-off of the Transaction shall remain unaffected.

VOCABULARY ASSISTANT

applicability *Anwendbarkeit* claims *Ansprüche* conclude *hier: abschließen* confidentiality *Vertraulichkeit* contractual penalty *Vertragsstrafe* in any event *in jedem Fall* in the event *für den Fall, dass* incur *verursachen* lump-sum amount *Pauschalbetrag* notification *Mitteilung* provisions *Bestimmungen* transfer *Übertragung* unaffected *unberührt*

Are the statements below true or false?

1 If the seller is already in discussion with a third party, he can't continue these discussions. ☐
2 If the seller breaks off discussions with the purchaser, he has the right to start discussions with a third party immediately. ☐
3 If the seller breaches the exclusivity clause, the purchaser is allowed claim compensation in addition to the EUR 100,000 contractual penalty. ☐
4 If the purchaser does not observe the terms of the confidentiality clause, the seller can break off the transaction without having to pay any compensation. ☐
5 If the purchaser breaks off the transaction, the seller can only claim a maximum compensation payment of EUR 50,000. ☐

12 Esskultur AG is planning to acquire a UK company. Have a meeting about a Letter of Intent.

Use some of the expressions for meetings in exercise 10.

PARTNER FILES
Partner A File 08, p. 73
Partner B File 08, p. 78

"Fairness Opinions" are assessments provided by banks which show whether the valuation of a company is fair. Read the article below.

Final Provisions

Regarding Fairness Opinions Pros Ask, What's Fair?

New research and a recent ruling from the SEC take aim at the conflicts inherent in fairness opinions

by Ken MacFadyen

A recent report has reignited *(neu aufflammen lassen)* the debate around fairness opinions with claims that conflicts of interest do in fact exist. The examination into what is fair is by no means new. But since 1985, when the Delaware Supreme Court ruled against Trans-Union Corp., decreeing *(entscheiden)* that the company's board was negligent *(fahrlässig)* in its sale, most public companies have sought out fairness opinions as a shield *(Schutz)* against litigation.

Questions, though, still surround what is motivating the banks providing these opinions. If they are indeed being brought in to "rubber stamp" *(routinemäßig absegnen)* a deal, then would it be good practice to impede *(hindern)* the deal's progress? Or, even worse, if the banks are involved in other parts of the transaction, such as the financing, would they risk those fees by declaring a transaction "unfair?"

According to a new report, fairness opinions are impacted *(berührt)* by these diverging *(auseinandergehend)* agendas. Rajesh Narayanan, (University of Georgia), co-authored the report with Anil Makhija, (Ohio State University). While he concedes *(einräumen)* that the research is a work in progress, Narayanan tells *M&A* that out of the deals the pair looked at (a sampling of 1,927 transactions), companies that didn't employ fairness opinions typically fetched higher premiums than those that had brought in outside help. On average, when banks provided an opinion, the target companies reached a premium that was 48 % above their share price going into the deal, versus a 54 % premium when no fairness opinion was provided. "The banks are brought in to find a price at which they can get the deal done," Narayanan says. "But they don't necessarily tell you if a company can find a better price."

Any solutions?

The SEC finally weighed in on *(einsteigen)* the debate, and after years of analysis, issued a concrete ruling (NASD Rule 2290) that broadly calls for more disclosure *(Preisgabe von Informationen)*. The directive now forces member firms to disclose if they will receive a "success fee" at the completion of the deal, and also make public whether or not they have had other relationships with the target company. The ruling also requires member firms to incorporate in writing *(schriftlich fixieren)* the procedures used to develop the opinion.

While more disclosure will help erase *(ausräumen)* some doubts surrounding fairness opinions, some critics feel the ruling will fall short of having any real impact. Narayanan, meanwhile, cites *(zitieren)* his research, noting that when fairness opinions were provided by "independent" advisers, the average merger premium was higher than deals that included opinions from banks with previous or ongoing relationships. However, Narayanan isn't ready to say independence should be required. "There is the chance that a current adviser, if they're intimately involved with the company, knows more about its true value."

Article from "Mergers&Acquisitions, (abridged)

Over to you

- Why do some people feel that banks don't always do a good job?
- What has the Securities and Exchange Commission (SEC) decided to do to improve things?
- What measures exist in your country for ensuring that a company is valued objectively?
- What remedies exist if a party feels that a valuation is too low or too high?

6 Risk managment and insolvency

Preamble

How can the following be a source of potential risk to a company?

RISK

- trade marks / patents
- warranties
- plant and equipment
- corporate compliance code
- company pension scheme
- employment legislation
- contracts with suppliers
- health and safety legislation

1 The business magazine "Fact File" regularly conducts interviews with entrepreneurs from different continents who have successfully set up businesses in Europe. Read the extract from an interview with Piet Forster from South Africa and put the questions back in the correct place.

a And you were happy to rely on your client's assurances?
b So had you already founded *Form and Function*, your office and hotel furniture business, in Cape Town?
c But not everything went to plan, did it?
d And the headquarters of the company have remained in Cape Town?
e And what made your products different?
f What brought you to Vienna?

Fact File ____________________ 1

PF Yes, we had.

Fact File ____________________ 2

PF Well, three things really. Firstly, they were ergonomically designed. Secondly, our furniture was based around a building block principle. All units could be taken apart and reassembled in different shapes to give customers maximum flexibility in their use of resources. Finally, the styling was light and uncomplicated.

Fact File ____________________ 3

PF Pure chance really. A lot of our customers in South Africa happened to be subsidiaries and branch offices of Austrian companies and they assured us that our products and design concept would definitely fill a gap in the market in Europe.

Fact File ____ 4

PF Not entirely, no. We hired an agency to do some market research. The findings looked promising, so we decided to open a branch office in Vienna – about five years ago.

Fact File ____ 5

PF Actually, no. Business began to look so promising in Europe that we registered the company in Austria as a limited and made our Cape Town office a branch. We also set up a European production facility outside Bregenz and acquired a timber processing company in Finland.

Fact File ____ 6

PF Not at all. We had a very difficult period a few years back. We could almost have gone under. You see, what happened ...

2 Piet says "We could almost have *gone under*." "*Go under*" is a phrasal verb. A lot of phrasal verbs are used in the context of insolvency. Have a look at the following newspaper report and match the phrasal verbs with their dictionary definitions below.

Skylark wiped out

by our financial affairs correspondent Hazel Watts

Skylark plc, the low-cost airline founded in the late 1990s, announced yesterday that it had gone into liquidation. This is the second European budget airline to **go under** in as many months. The announcement followed weeks of speculation that the airline's creditors were unwilling to **bail** it **out** with extra cash. "The company will now be **wound up** as a matter of urgency," said Jonathan Mills, Skylark's CEO. This will be little comfort to Skylark's unsecured creditors, some of whom will have to **write off** considerable sums.

Skylark had been the big success story of the past decade. It quickly rose to become the leading player in the budget airline market with a spectacular series of hostile takeovers. Criticism of Skylark's sharp business practices was growing, however, and the decision of the OFT to impose a £50 m fine for price fixing **set** the company **back** financially towards the end of last year. In order to make this payment, Skylark was forced to **draw on** its capital reserves and to borrow as well. When the markets suffered a downturn earlier this year, the airline found itself overstretched. The crunch came when it tried to raise the £20 m it needed to **ward off** insolvency. So bad was the scale of the problem at this stage, according to inside sources, that the banks refused to **put up** what, by the standards of the airline industry, is a relatively modest sum.

Example *ward off* to prevent something from causing harm to someone

1 ____________ to rescue

2 ____________ to obtain money from an existing source

3 ____________ to delay or impede the progress of something

4 ____________ to become bankrupt

5 ____________ to provide money for an enterprise

6 ____________ to cancel the record of a bad debt

7 ____________ to dissolve a company

8 ____________ to destroy, eliminate

3 Now practise phrasal verbs with a partner.

PARTNER FILES
Partner A File 09, p. 73
Partner B File 09, p. 78

4 The story of Form and Function's difficult period begins a few years ago with an e-mail from the Finance Director, Jana Burzinski, about risk assessment within the company. Read the e-mail and answer the questions below.

Delete Reply Reply All Forward Print

From: Jana Burzinski «jana.burzinski@formandfunction.at»
To: Piet Forster «piet.forster@formandfunction.at»
Subject: Risk Management

Dear Piet

Just a quick e-mail to confirm that I have completed my check on the following:

- Directors' liability insurance
- Company accident and injury liability insurance
- Buildings and contents insurance against fire, flood, theft, accidental damage etc.
- Compliance with statutory health and safety requirements
- Compliance with statutory requirements regarding dangerous substances

Everything is up to date and in order.

I am increasingly concerned, however, that our risk management procedures are too focused on questions of health and safety, and insurance. With your permission, I'd like to carry out a fuller risk management audit covering commercial, financial and legal risks.

The commercial and financial risks we should look into are e.g. over-reliance on large clients, exchange rate risks (given that we are beginning to export outside of the euro zone) and the fact that the current value of our production facility in Bregenz is possibly lower than the level of the bank loan secured upon it.

In order to assess our legal risks I would need to involve *Wenger, Holzmann und Brandt*, our lawyers here in Vienna. I understand that Florian Wenger specializes in risk management issues.

I appreciate that this audit will take some time and will cost money. Nevertheless, I feel strongly that we need to have a much clearer picture of our exposure to risk.

Let me know what you think.

Best regards

Jana

VOCABULARY ASSISTANT

compliance with *Einhaltung von*
dangerous substances *Schadstoffe*
exposure to risk *Risikoanfälligkeit*
over-reliance on *eine zu große Abhängigkeit von*
statutory requirements *gesetzliche Bestimmungen*

1 Why is Jana unhappy about the company's current risk management procedures?

____

2 In what ways could the three commercial or financial risks mentioned by Jana cause problems for the company in future?

____

3 What would be Florian Wenger's role?

____

13

5 Later that day Jana finds a message on her voicemail. Listen and decide which of the statements is correct?

1 When Piet says, "I see where you're coming from", he means
  a I understand your position on this issue.
  b I agree with you on this issue.
  c It is clear to me that you want to discuss this issue.

2 a Piet has no problem with Jana's suggestion.
  b Piet does not want to carry out this audit.
  c Piet has some reservations about this audit.

3 a Piet tells Jana to go ahead.
  b Piet wants more information before he can decide.
  c Piet says that he doesn't want to go into detail at this stage.

6 In the course of carrying out his share of the risk assessment task Florian Wenger finds that he is particularly concerned by the following contract clauses:

2. Commencement, Duration of Lease, Transfer

(1) The lease shall commence on the day of transfer in accordance with section 2(2).
(2) The transfer shall take place on 1st November 2…
(5) The lease shall end five years after the day on which it commenced.
(6) The lease shall be automatically extended by a further five years unless the Lessee formally waives its right to this extension. Notification of its intention to waive this right must be made to the Lessor in writing at least twelve months prior to the end of the lease pursuant to section 2(5).

5. Rent price adjustment

(3) The rent payable shall be adjusted automatically if the consumer price index for Austria (basis in year 1 = 100), as published by the Federal Statistical Office, rises or falls by ten points compared with the value at the start of the lease or at the time of the previous adjustment of the rent payable.

3. Compensation

For the loss of his/her employment the Employer shall pay to the Employee a compensation of three monthly salaries per year of employment. The compensation shall be paid in addition to the salary owed by the Employer until the Termination Date pursuant to sec. 2 para. (1) of this agreement. The claim to the payment of the compensation shall be inheritable.

6. Sale price adjustment

(1) The base purchase price increases by the amount by which, as of 31st December of the first full calendar year following signature of this agreement, the value of the working capital – as defined in section 4.1 above – is greater than the amount of EUR 750,000. Analogously, the base purchase price is reduced by the amount by which the value of the working capital, as of 31st December of the first full calendar year following this agreement, is lower than the amount of EUR 750,000.

VOCABULARY ASSISTANT

adjust *anpassen*
analogously *analog hierzu*
consumer price index (CPI) *Verbraucherpreisindex* inheritable *vererbbar* lessee *Mieter* lessor *Vermieter*
prior to *before* working capital *Umsatzkapital, Betriebskapital*

Discuss the following points.

1 What kind of legal agreements do the above clauses come from? Label each of the contracts.
2 In what way might each of these clauses represent a potential risk to Form and Function GmbH?

14

7 Now listen to part of the meeting between Piet Forster, Jana Burzinski and Florian Wenger and see if you guessed the three legal agreements correctly.

VOCABULARY ASSISTANT

capital reserve *Kapitalreserve* challenge *anfechten* deductions *Abgaben* disadvantageous *nicht vorteilhaft* gross *brutto* insert *einfügen* lay off *betriebsbedingt kündigen* leasehold agreement *Mietvertrag* premises *Geschäftsräume* price adjustment *Preisanpassung* profit allocation *Gewinnverteilung* redundancy clause *Kündigungsklausel* renew *erneuern* statutory amount *gesetzlich bestimmter Betrag* works council agreement *Betriebsratsvereinbarung*

Listen again and complete the table.

Clause / Legal Document	Risk	Action necessary
2 / ____________ ____________ 5 / ____________ ____________		
3 / ____________ ____________		
6 / ____________ ____________		

USEFUL PHRASES

We can add emphasis to what we say in the following ways:

1 by stressing a particular word e.g. I ***will*** try to keep it straightforward.
2 by adding the auxiliary 'do' e.g. I **did** find ...
3 by restructuring the statement, "Clause 5 is the problem" into "**It's** clause 5 **that** is the problem."
4 by changing the statement, "I would recommend that you allocate ..." into "**What** I would recommend **is** that you allocate ..."
5 by moving certain negative or near negative adverbs or adverbial phrases e.g. **never**, **under no circumstances**, **at no time**, **on no account**, **seldom** to the beginning of the sentence.
Therefore, "You should not, under any circumstances, just allow the lease to be extended." becomes "**Under no circumstances should you** just allow the lease to be extended."
When we use this structure the subject and verb invert i.e. "you should" becomes "should you".

NB When the main verb is in the *simple present* or *simple past* the following happens:
"My client never claimed he was a partner in the company." becomes "Never **did** my client **claim** he was a ..."

8 Florian sometimes tries to add emphasis to what he says. Look at the explanations in the Useful Phrases box and then rebuild the sentences below to make them more emphatic.

1 My client was not at any time made aware of the true financial circumstances of your client's company when he signed the contract. (At no time ... .)
2 One seldom comes across an employment contract with as many loopholes as this. (Seldom ...)
3 The whole question of misrepresentation interests me in this case. (It ... .)
4 The members of this union find it particularly unfair that the company is considering cuts after such a successful year. (What ....)
5 I find it suspicious that the company in this case was registered in the Cayman Islands. (What ... .)
6 The rest of the clause is fine. However, the last sentence is open to interpretation. (It ...)

9 About 18 months later the following report appears in the financial press.

Fuller's Construction plc digs itself into a hole

by our financial affairs correspondent Hazel Watts

Mr. Gareth Jenkins, the chairman of Fuller's Construction plc, announced yesterday that the company's board of directors had petitioned Sussex County Court for a winding up order. A liquidator has already been appointed to wind up what is one of the UK's market leaders in the construction of hotels and residential homes for the elderly. "In view of the collapse in orders we have experienced and the insolvency of two of our major clients, we were advised by our lawyers that no other course of action was open to us. All attempts to involve our creditors in a debt restructuring plan, which would have reduced the monthly cost of the company's loan repayments, had failed," explained Mr. Jenkins.

Not only the financial markets were caught unawares by the news. Brian Harrington, the chairman of British Brick Ltd, expressed concern at the impact of this insolvency on his company. Other key suppliers to Fuller's Construction, who may be affected, are understood to be Thermaglass plc, manufacturers of double glazing, and Form and Function GmbH, the Austrian-based furniture designers. Investment analysts ...

1 What two reasons does the chairman give for the company's insolvency?

____

____

2 What role did the company's creditors play in the insolvency?

____

____

3 What does this insolvency have to do with Form and Function GmbH?

____

____

15

10 Now listen to a meeting in which Piet Forster, Jana Burzinski and Florian Wenger discuss the implications of the insolvency for Form and Function. Are the following statements true or false?

1 An administration order and a winding-up order are basically the same. ☐
2 The person appointed by the court is going to try to sell Fuller Construction's assets. ☐
3 Jana only knew that Fuller's construction was experiencing payment difficulties at the beginning of the month. ☐
4 Form and Function GmbH would be regarded as an unsecured creditor. ☐
5 Florian is confident that Form and Function GmbH can get all its furniture back. ☐
6 Jana doesn't think this will be possible. ☐
7 It's possible that Form and Function will suffer a loss of 1.5 million. ☐
8 Jana thinks that some of Form and Function's non-core activities may not survive this crisis. ☐

VOCABULARY ASSISTANT

administration order *Konkurseröffnungsbeschluss*
appoint *ernennen* charge *Pfandrecht* charge holder *Pfandhalter*
compulsory liquidation *Zwangsauflösung*
creditor *Gläubige(r)* default on payment *Zahlungsverpflichtungen nicht nachkommen*
instalment *Rate* issue *erlassen* knock-down price *stark reduzierter Preis*
off-load *abladen* petition a court *etwas beim Gericht beantragen*
preferential *bevorzugt* realize assets *Vermögen veräußern* secured *gesichert*
service debts *Zins- und Tilgungszahlungen leisten* unsecured *ungesichert*
voluntary redundancy *freiwilliges Ausscheiden* winding-up order *Liquidationsbeschluss*

11 A lawyer discusses an insolvency case with a client. Work with a partner.

PARTNER FILES
Partner A File 10, p. 74
Partner B File 10, p. 79

DID YOU KNOW?

In the UK, as in Germany, it is illegal for a company to continue trading once it has become **insolvent**. In both jurisdictions, however, there is now a greater emphasis on **rescuing** than on **liquidating** the company or **winding** it **up**. Accordingly, there is a distinction drawn between a company being in ***administration*** and in ***liquidation***. These two procedures are carried out by an ***administrator*** or a ***liquidator*** accordingly. The administrator has the task of keeping the company going; the liquidator has the job of winding the company up and **realizing** its **assets** in order to satisfy its **creditors** as far as possible. This work is often done by **Insolvency Practitioners**, who are usually specially qualified accountants. If the liquidator is appointed directly by the court, s/he is called the **Official Receiver (OR)**.

In Germany-speaking countries, the ***Insolvenzverwalter*** is appointed by a court and has to determine whether the company can be rescued.

In the USA, companies, file with the **bankruptcy court**. The two procedures that are broadly analogous to administration and liquidation are called **Chapter 11** (administration) and **Chapter 7** (liquidation) of the US **Bankruptcy Code**. For example, a company "goes Chapter 11" or it "goes Chapter 7".

12 Read this excerpt from the booklet "A Guide for Creditors", published by the Insolvency Service at The Department of Trade and Industry in the UK and fill in the gaps.

asset • ~~creditor~~ • distribute • preferential • repayment • secured • unsecured

Creditors – Order of priority

The rights of a creditor who holds a fixed charge, or security, on assets (such as a mortgage) to sell the asset to recover their debt are not affected by insolvency. The chargeholder (______[1] creditor) is the first to get paid when the ______[2] is sold. Any surplus will be handed over to the trustee/ liquidator.

When all the assets available to unsecured creditors have been realized, the trustee/liquidator will ______[3] the proceeds in a strict order of priority as follows:

1. The fees and charges of the liquidation/bankruptcy.
2. Debts due to ______[4] creditors,. These debts are set out in the Insolvency Act 1986 and include wages owed in the four months before the date of the insolvency order and contributions to occupational pension schemes.
3. All unsecured creditors.
4. Any interest payable on debts.
5. In company cases, the shareholders.

Therefore, ______[5] creditors will usually only be paid when the fees and charges of the insolvency procedures and the claims of secured and preferential creditors have been paid. If full ______[6] of claims is not possible, payments are made to creditors by way of a dividend in proportion to the value of each claim.

13 Read the end of Piet Forster's interview with Fact File and fill the gaps.

acquisition • debts • insolvent • lease • loss • severance

Fact File So how close were you to becoming ______[1] at that time?

PF Well, not nearly as close as we would have been. You see, we implemented most of the risk management measures suggested at the time and I'm glad we did. If we hadn't renegotiated the ______[2] on our business premises and our staff ______[3] arrangements, and if we hadn't put aside capital to cover for the additional sums that arose due to our ______[4] of *Finnwood*, our financial situation would have been much tighter. It wouldn't have been as easy to finance the necessary redundancies and to restructure our ______[5]. As it was, we were able to absorb the ______[6] of 1.5 million euros and we haven't looked back since.

USEFUL PHRASES

In his interview with *Fact File* Piet Forster looks back at the past and considers scenarios that were a possibility at the time, but that didn't happen. We often do this when we talk about mistakes we made or mistakes we avoided making. The structure works as follows:

If we **hadn't implemented** those risk management measures, we **would have gone** under.

The logic of the statement is that they **did** implement the risk management measures and as a result they **didn't** go under.

14 Rewrite the following statements.

Examples Our client withheld vital evidence so we lost the case.
If our client hadn't withheld vital evidence, we wouldn't have lost the case.

The core business was healthy, so the Insolvency Practitioner didn't wind the company up.
If the core business hadn't been healthy, the Insolvency Practitioner would have wound the company up.

1 The new machine in the company's warehouse was paid for, so it was part of the insolvency estate.

____

2 The bank secured its loan against assets of the company, so it got its money back.

____

3 The creditors had no confidence in the company's ability to pay, so they petitioned the court to make a winding-up order.

____

____

4 The directors didn't delay in registering the company insolvent, so they weren't guilty of an offence.

____

5 The company got into a lot of speculative ventures, so its core business was exposed to risk.

____

6 It was a company with limited liability, so the members' personal assets were not at risk.

____

15 Choose from the topics in the list and tell your partner what happened. Try to finish with a sentence like the ones you practised above.

- a case that went badly because the judge made a strange ruling
- a difficult client or difficult board of management decision
- a failure to negotiate an out-of-court settlement
- a course in your studies which, contrary to your expectations, turned out to be useful
- something important that you noticed in a contract but nearly missed
- a case in which your client didn't tell you something important

Final Provisions

Look at the definition of Individual Voluntary Arrangements (IVAs) and then read the article from *The Times* newspaper below.

Individual voluntary arrangements (IVA)
An individual voluntary arrangement is an alternative to bankruptcy. It is a formal agreement with your creditors to pay part or all of your debts.

Lenders write off a record £1.4bn of IVA debt

by Graham Searjeant, Financial Editor

Lenders have written off *(abschreiben)* a record £1.4 billion this year as more consumers than ever dish *(loswerden)* their debts but keep their homes by entering into Individual Voluntary Arrangements (IVAs) with their creditors. An analysis by KPMG, the accountancy firm, has found that about 45,000 people have entered IVAs during this year — double the figure for the previous year. People applying for IVAs, now overwhelmingly consumers, had average debts of £52,000, but on average they have offered to repay only 39 per cent to their creditors.

Banks and other credit institutions have expressed increasing alarm at the unregulated spread of IVAs among consumers but have received little sympathy from the government or debt counselling bodies, which blame them for lax *(nicht streng)* lending standards.

IVAs were introduced by the Thatcher Government as a measure to encourage more people to take the risk of founding new businesses. If the business failed, an IVA would be less brutal and carry less stigma because it has fewer restrictions than bankruptcy. In the early years, IVAs helped about 2,000 people a year to cope with business failure. Recently, however, the use of IVAs has radically changed.

Steve Treharne, KPMG's head of personal insolvency, said: "Typically, the sort of debts we have seen being dealt with by IVAs this year are personal loans, credit card balances and other forms of buy-now-pay-later unsecured loans. Most of the money is borrowed to meet current expenditure, including lifestyle elements such as holidays, rather than to acquire assets or to fund a business."

(abridged)

Over to you

- Do IVAs, in your view, provide a necessary safety net to individuals who have got into debt or do they simply encourage irresponsible personal spending?
- Does your country have anything comparable to IVAs?
- Is it necessary to impose tighter credit restrictions on banks and credit card comparies?

Test yourself!

See how much legal vocabulary you have learned.
Use the clues to complete the crossword puzzle.

Across

3 the pay and benefits from your employer in return for the work you do
5 shareholders' capital
7 If you act in accordance with a contract, then you ... with it.
8 You ... a provision in a contract if you wish to base your case on it.
10 to take legal action against another party
12 a type of firm without a separate legal identity to which two or more people belong
17 a document explaining the constitution of a company and its internal decision-making procedures
18 A provision or an entire contract that places an obligation on a party can be described as ... .
19 If you no longer wish to make use of a right, you can ... it.
20 someone who works for themselves but not in a registered trade
21 a patent holder
23 a violation of an intellectual property right
25 the clause containing factors that prevent performance in a contract and that are beyond control
28 a change to a legal document
29 A liquidator is said to ... an asset if he or she sells it in order to be able to pay creditors.

Down

1 another word for earlier or before
2 a decision or intention agreed by shareholders at a formal meeting
4 A company that is no longer able to meet its financial obligations is ... .
6 to create new shares and offer them for sale
9 in the case of insolvency this is a type of creditor, e.g. an employee
11 If a sum of money is paid in regular smaller amounts, each of these amounts is an ... .
13 payments made to authors or composers based on the sales of their work
14 detailed information about the features and properties of a product
15 A contract in which a fundamental prerequisite of a contract hasn't been fulfilled, is ... .
16 having the right to something
20 the legal word meaning "to found" a company
22 any form of collateral for a loan
24 A company which others are aiming to take over is a ... company.
26 another word for agree or agreement
27 things that belong to a company or a person

1
2
3
4
5
6
7
8
9
10
11
12
13
14
15
16
17
18
19
20
21
22
23
24
25
26
27
28
29

Partner A

Partner files

UNIT 1, Exercise 10 File 01

Part 1

In Part 1 you play the role of two separate clients who would like to have advice from a lawyer. Explain your situation to your partner.

Case 1

You have just lost your job at a company that manufactures washing machines. You understand a lot about washing machines and you want to go into business as a repair man.

Your lawyer will give you advice. You don't really want to form a limited company. Give some reasons.

Case 2

You are a partner in a small ordinary or general partnership that offers translation and proofreading services. One of your partners has just read about a case in which 75,000 annual statements for the Annual General Meeting of a major DAX company had to be reprinted because the translators missed out an important table of figures. At 3.00 per copy, this meant a claim of 225,000 against the translating agency. In addition, there were postage costs amounting to a further 55,000. Your partnership is acquiring some major corporate clients and worried about liability. You know that if a large claim exceeds the limit of your liability insurance, your personal assets will be at risk.

Your lawyer will give you some advice. You feel strongly that it might be necessary to convert your partnership into another legal form.

Part 2

Now it is your turn to play the role of a lawyer and advise two separate clients about forming a company.

Case 1

Listen to your client. Explain to him/her the available options: bringing in a new shareholder / borrowing money from the bank / forming a public limited company and issuing shares. Basically, you feel that organic growth might be best – just using the company's capital reserves to expand step by step.

Case 2

Listen to your client. Explain to him/her the available options. On the whole, you feel that it might be best for your client to work as a freelancer with his/her own agency and to employ the two younger colleagues – maybe with the chance of a partnership if things go well.

UNIT 1, Exercise 14 File 02

Explain the procedure for registering a private limited company or a partnership in your jurisdiction.

UNIT 2, Exercise 4 File 03

Task 1

You are an employment lawyer in Switzerland advising English-speaking employees at a Swiss company. Below are some clauses from a contract of employment. Your partner wishes to consult you about three problems at work. Listen carefully and then give him/her your opinion. When you refer to a clause, use the **useful phrases** in the box on p. 19.

1 Place of work

The place of work is the business premises of the Company in Berne. Work-related trips (client visits, trade fairs, exhibitions, projects etc.) may require work in places other than the aforementioned premises. However, such places of work shall always be of a temporary nature.

2.1 Working hours and location

Berne office

The work must be carried out during the period 8.00 a.m. to 6.00 p.m. (Mondays to Thursdays) and 7.30 a.m. to 5.30 p.m. (Fridays). The core hours are as follows: 9.30 a.m. to 4.00 p.m. (Monday to Thursdays) and 9.00 a.m. to 3.30 p.m. (Fridays).

3.2 Overtime

As a rule, the Employee is entitled to receive compensation for overtime in the following way: free time for one-third of the overtime worked and payment for two-thirds. Compensation for overtime exclusively by payment or exclusively by free time is possible following agreement with the line manager. The line manager may not withhold consent unreasonably.

4.1 Annual leave entitlement

The Employer grants 30 days' paid holiday a year on the basis of a five-day week. The statutory school holidays shall be made available as a matter of priority to employees with children of school age and employees whose partners or spouses are obliged by reason of their profession to take their annual leave during the statutory school holiday period. The employee is entitled to three weeks' continuous holiday (15 working days).

Task 2

Swap roles with your partner. You are now an employee and your partner is a lawyer. You wish to consult your partner about the following three problems at work. Read each problem out loud and then make a note of the advice you are given.

4. "I rang in sick on Friday morning and the company received my doctor's note on the following Wednesday. When I got back to work, my boss was very nice but she did ask me to make sure in future that I hand in my sick note on time. I thought I had. Am I really in the wrong here?"

5. "I went on a two-week holiday to Spain last month. While I was there I became ill and I went to a Spanish doctor. He treated me and told me to stay in bed for two or three days. He also wrote a short note – in English – for my doctor back in Berne, telling him what medication he had prescribed. I was ill for three days and I would like to have this time counted as sickness not holiday. My boss disagrees. He says I haven't got a proper sick note. Who is right here?"

6. "I'm going on holiday to India and have to have a hepatitis vaccination at the doctor's. The doctor usually does these vaccinations on Thursday afternoons between 3 and 4 pm. I told my boss I would have to leave work early and he said I could but I would have to take half a day's leave. Surely, he isn't right!"

UNIT 2, Exercise 11 — File 04

You are the solicitor acting for Intelligent Solutions Ltd. Your position is as follows:

- It would be Cathy O'Brien's job to coordinate Softline's software design projects with external partners. Some of these external partners are direct competitors of Intelligent Solutions Ltd. So there is a clear risk to your client.
- You don't want to block Cathy O'Brien's move to Softline, but you will if there is no other way to protect your client's commercial interests. What is more, Cathy O'Brien's contract allows you to block her move to Softline for two years.
- Intelligent Solutions Ltd has told Cathy O'Brien to stay at home during her period of notice. The cost of paying her to do nothing is EUR 20,000. In addition, there is a further EUR 30,000 necessary to cover the cost of external consultants who have to be called in to do her work. You would like Softline to cover these costs.
- To compensate you for the risk that know-how may pass to a competitor you would like a payment from Softline of a further EUR 100,000.

UNIT 3, Exercise 12 — File 05

1 Read out the definitions of legal words below, but don't read out the word in bold. See if your partner can give you the word you are looking for.

2 Now listen to your partner's definitions. Try to provide the missing word.

If performance is not good enough, we can say that it is … . **unsatisfactory**	If two parties cannot find common ground in a dispute, we can say that they are … . **irreconcilable**
If some important clauses are missing from a contract, then we can say that the contract is … . **incomplete**	If an export licence expires, then this licence cannot be used because it is … . **invalid**
If the purchaser says that he plans to place an order for some goods but he still hasn't actually placed the order, we can say that this order is … . **unconfirmed**	If one party reacts to a situation in a way that is excessive, this party's behaviour can be said to be … . **unreasonable**

UNIT 3, Exercise 13 File 06

Task 1
You are a client and you go to a lawyer with the following problem. Just give a brief overview of the problem. Then let the lawyer ask you questions to find out the details.

Overview
I'm trying to sell my house at the moment and I'm having problems with a prospective buyer. He says that I am bound by an offer which I accepted earlier. I think he is wrong.

Details
My house is valued at around EUR 340,000. I put it on the market three months ago and invited offers in the region of EUR 340,000. I was visited by a prospective buyer, Mr. Blue. He had a look at the house and found some things that needed to be repaired or improved (two defective windows / a problem with the light in the cellar / the locks on the front and back door / part of the fence round the garden / some tiles on the roof). I agreed with him and offered to sell my house to him for EUR 320,000. He asked for a day to think about my offer. He then contacted me a day later and offered EUR 300,000. I told him that his offer was too low for me and rejected it. A week later I received another offer from Mr. Blue of EUR 320,000. By this time I was already in negotiations with another prospective buyer, Mrs. Green. She was really interested in the house and there was a good chance that we would agree on a sales price of around EUR 325,000 or even EUR 330,000. I contacted Mr. Blue and told him I wasn't interested in his offer. Now he has sent me a letter telling me I am bound by the original offer I made to him of EUR 320,000. He's not right, is he?

Task 2
You are a lawyer. A client comes to you with a problem. He or she is going to give you a brief overview of the problem. Then you must ask questions to get all the necessary details. Try to use some of the language in the **useful phrases** box on page 35. Finally, give your client some advice about what to do.

UNIT 4, Exercise 12 File 07

You are an attorney-at-law, acting on behalf of Global Music Inc. (PUBLISHER). You are planning to enter into an exclusive copyright agreement with Mr. Billy Ratt (COMPOSER), a popular rap music artist. You have sent Mr. Ratt's attorneys a draft version of the proposed agreement, but they are unhappy with the following clauses:

1. COMPOSER … hereby undertakes to assign, transfer and deliver to PUBLISHER … the whole of the copyright for all countries of the world … in and to such music and lyrics written heretofore by COMPOSER insofar as such copyright is not held by third parties.

2. COMPOSER … will endeavour to deliver a minimum of ten compositions, each of which compromising three minutes of music on average, every year for the duration of this Agreement.

4. The rights of PUBLISHER include the right … to assign in whole or in part the compositions hereunder …

5. The term of the Agreement shall be for a period of three years from the date hereof. PUBLISHER shall have the option to renew this Agreement for a further period of three years.

8. PUBLISHER agrees to pay fees and royalties in respect of the compositions acquired hereunder to COMPOSER as follows:

iii) 12.5% of net receipts including the licensing of compositions for use in films, television programmes and commercials.

10. The royalty and fee statements shall be made up to June 30th and December 31st in each year and shall include all receipts by PUBLISHER in that period. Such statements will be sent to COMPOSER within 28 days of the relevant date and shall be accompanied by a remittance for the amounts which are shown by the statement to be due and payable.

You are quite happy with these clauses as they stand. Before you start the role-play, if possible, work with someone who has the same role. Try to think of some good reasons for keeping the draft clauses as they are.

During the role-play, be prepared to listen carefully to the arguments of Mr. Ratt's attorneys. It will be necessary to make some amendments to the draft clauses, but try to get the best possible deal for your client.

UNIT 5, Exercise 12 File 08

The company *Esskultur* AG is planning the acquisition of a UK company called Fusion Food.

You are a solicitor acting for *Esskultur* AG. Here are some clauses from the draft version of the Letter of Intent (LOI). Have a meeting with the solicitor representing Fusion Food. Your aim is to reach agreement with them about the precise wording of the LOI. Your position is set out below.

4 Exclusivity
(1) Beginning with the signing of this Letter of Intent until six months after the end of the due diligence period, the Seller shall not hold any discussions, either directly or indirectly, with any third party about the transfer of the Shares or of the Company's business operations. The Seller shall end any ongoing discussions.

2) The exclusivity ends in any event upon the signature of the share purchase agreement or if one of the parties breaks off from the Transaction pursuant to clause 7(1).

(3) In the event the Seller breaches the exclusivity, it shall pay a contractual penalty in the amount of EUR 100,000 to the Purchaser. Further claims of the Purchaser shall remain unaffected. The contractual penalty shall not be payable, if binding contracts are concluded between the parties.

7 Binding Effect
(1) This Letter of Intent does not create any obligation to carry out the Transaction. Both parties shall be entitled to break off from the Transaction at any time before the share purchase agreement is signed, without having to give any reason. The notification of breaking-off must be in writing.

(2) The breaking-off shall not affect the applicability of the provisions in 4(3) and 7(3) of this Letter of Intent; these provisions shall remain binding.

(3) If the Seller breaks off the Transaction, it shall pay a lump-sum amount of EUR 100,000 to the Purchaser as compensation for its necessary expenses incurred in connection with the Transaction, unless the breaking-off is because of a breach by the Purchaser of the confidentiality obligation. If the Purchaser breaks off the Transaction, it shall pay a lump-sum amount of EUR 50,000 to the Seller as compensation for its necessary expenses, unless the breaking-off is because of a breach by the Seller of the exclusivity or confidentiality obligations. More extensive claims resulting from the breaking-off of the Transaction shall remain unaffected.

Your position

Clause 4.1 is helpful because it gives your client confidence in the seriousness of *Fusion Food's* intentions.

A contractual penalty of EUR 100,000 in 4.3 is realistic. Your client will have to invest a lot of money in due diligence and the penalty clause is a guarantee against *Fusion Food* wasting his time.

Esskultur AG should have the right to make further claims against *Fusion Food* (4.3) if it can prove that it really has incurred these extra costs.

According to clause 7.3 *Fusion Food* should be entitled to lower compensation. Normally the seller doesn't invest as much money in due diligence as the purchaser.

Follow up

Present to the class any changes you have agreed to make to the wording of the Letter of Intent.

UNIT 6, EXERCISE 3 File 09

1 Read out the sentences below but don't read out the phrasal verb in bold in parentheses. See if your partner can find the word you are looking for.

- The investors are prepared to **BLANK** 10 m euros of capital for this project, but the board of management is asking for more. (**put up**)
- I accept that ABC Ltd owes you 50,000 euros. But they've gone bankrupt, so I think you may have to **BLANK** this debt **BLANK**. (**write off**)
- The company cannot recover. I would advise you to **BLANK** it **BLANK**. (**wind up**)
- As I see it, your company will have to **BLANK** its reserves to cover its losses. (**draw on**)

2 Now listen to your partner's sentences. Try to provide the missing word.

UNIT 6, EXERCISE 11 File 10

You are an insolvency lawyer. Prior to your first meeting, your client, Mr. Ranjit Singh, sent to you the following information about his current assets and liabilities. All the sums of money are in euros.

Liabilities		*Assets*	
Banks		*Flat*	*110,000*
Bank loan	*25,000*	*Receivables (unpaid invoices for party service and events)*	*8,000*
Mortgage (on flat)	*85,000*	*Inventory (kitchen equipment/ furniture)*	*10,000*
Staff			
Part-time employees	*6,000*		
Other creditors			
Utilities	*2,500*		
Landlord of premises	*6,500*		
Suppliers of fresh food	*2,500*		
Telephone / Internet	*500*		
Tax authorities	*18,000*		
Total	*146,000*	*Total*	*128,000*

Talk to him and find out:

- his career history
- the nature of his business
- location of business
- legal status of the business
- start-up capital needed
- source of the capital
- reason for business difficulties
- if he is currently servicing his loan and mortgage debts

Advise him on the following:

- How bad is his financial situation?
- Should he register himself insolvent?
- Is it possible to save his home?
- Are there other solutions available?

After you have finished the activity, be prepared to tell the rest of the class what advice you gave to your client.

Partner B

Partner files

UNIT 1, Exercise 10 File 01

Part 1
In Part 1 you play the role of a lawyer and advise two separate clients about forming a company.

Case 1
Listen to your client. Discuss with him/her the available options. Generally, you favour a limited company because washing machines can go wrong and cause thousands in damage.

Case 2
Listen to your client. Discuss with him/her the available options. Generally, you think your client shouldn't overreact. Good liability insurance and good quality assurance procedures should be sufficient.

Part 2
Now it is your turn to play the role of two separate clients who would like to have advice from a lawyer. Explain your situation to your partner.

Case 1
You are one of three shareholder/directors of a successful private limited company specializing in solar cell technology. You would like to expand, but are worried about overstretching the company financially. You are also worried about losing management control of the company if you go public. The problem is that you don't have much choice but to expand. Your clients are demanding a wider range of products and higher volumes. They may lose confidence in your company if it doesn't grow.

Your lawyer will give you some advice. You feel that you must have a solution that gives you the option to expand quickly if necessary.

Case 2
You have worked as an employee in a large architectural partnership for ten years. You were hoping to be made a partner but this is now not very likely. You feel that you have good references to make a success of your own business. There is also some money in your family which you can use as start-up capital. You have two colleagues who are in the same situation as you, but they have fewer years' experience. They are talented and you all work well together. However, they have no capital which they could bring into a partnership.

Your lawyer will give you some advice. You feel that you would like to have these two colleagues on board as partners. How else can you persuade them to leave their current jobs?

UNIT 1, Exercise 14 File 02

Explain the advantages and/or disadvantages of one of the legal structures in the examples below.

a A firm decides to remain a private limited company even though it has a turnover in billions of euros and could raise substantial sums of money if it went public.

b An entrepreneur decides to buy a "shelf" company *(Mantelgesellschaft)* rather than form a new one.

UNIT 2, Exercise 4 File 03

Task 1
You are an English-speaking employee in a Swiss company. You wish to consult your lawyer about the following three problems at work. Read each problem out to your partner and then make a note of the advice you are given.

1. "I normally work in the Berne office but the company has set up a project group in the offices of a cooperation partner in Lucerne and now wants to send me there for the third week in a row. I asked my line manager how long my presence in Lucerne was going to be for and she said she didn't know. Can she keep sending me to Lucerne for as long as she wants?"

2. "I have 36 hours on my overtime account at the moment. I'm trying to save for a holiday and I'd like to be paid for all 36 hours. My line manager says that I should accept payment for 12 hours and that I should take the other 24 hours as free time. He says that he doesn't have time to discuss the matter further. Do I have to accept this? "

3. "A colleague told me that she can take her summer leave during the school holidays because she has children aged 8 and 10. I haven't got any children, but when I told her that my live-in boyfriend is a school teacher, she said that this doesn't count. Is she right?"

Task 2
Swap roles with your partner. You are now a lawyer. Below are some clauses from a contract of employment. Your partner wishes to consult you about three problems at work. Listen carefully and then give him/her your opinion. When you refer to a clause, use the **useful phrases** in the box on p. 19.

5 Sickness during annual leave

In the event that an employee becomes sick while on annual leave, the sick days covered by a doctor's note shall not be counted as annual leave.

6 Public duties and appointments with authorities

As a rule, such appointments will be either court appointments (e.g. being summoned to appear in court as a witness or as an expert,) or medical checks required by the Employer or made necessary by a business trip in the course of the Employee's duties to an overseas location for which certain vaccinations (e.g. tetanus, yellow fever, hepatitis) may be necessary. If the Employee can demonstrate that it is not possible for such appointments to be made outside of the core working times, the Employer must grant him paid time off in order to enable these appointments to be kept.

7 Marriage

The Employer grants one day's paid special leave for marriage involving immediate relatives (i.e. son/daughter, father/mother, brother/sister).

8.2 Inability to work due to sickness

In all cases of the employee being unable to work due to sickness the line manager must be informed immediately. A doctor's note must be produced no later than on the fourth calendar day following the commencement of the period of sickness.

UNIT 2, Exercise 11 — File 04

You are the solicitor representing Softline. Your position is as follows:

- You don't want Intelligent Solutions Ltd. to block Cathy O'Brien's move to your client. You think that the legal situation here isn't 100 % clear, but you accept that Intelligent Solutions Ltd has a case.
- Intelligent Solutions Ltd is not allowing Cathy O'Brien to work during her period of notice. You understand the reason for this and you accept that it is costing Intelligent Solutions Ltd money to keep her at home at the moment. Softline would be prepared to pay something here – maybe EUR 15,000 or 20,000.
- If Intelligent Solutions Ltd claims further compensation, you are not prepared to pay.
- Intelligent Solutions Ltd is a very good, innovative company. You are prepared to enter into new co-operation agreements with them.
- You are prepared to discuss systems and safeguards to prevent confidential information passing from Cathy O'Brien to third parties.

UNIT 3, Exercise 12 — File 05

1 Your partner is going to read out the definitions of some words. Listen and try to provide the missing word.

2 Read out the definitions of legal words below but don't read out the word in bold. See if your partner can give you the word you are looking for.

If the wrong number of pieces was delivered to the purchaser, we can say that the quantity delivered was … . **incorrect**	If a clause in a contract cannot stay as it is because the law has been changed, we can say that this clause is now … **ineffective**
In a dispute an arbitrator is not allowed to favour one party or the other. He must be … **impartial**	A severance clause ensures that, if one clause has to be changed, the other clauses remain … . **unaffected**
If it was impossible to know that a certain event e.g. a strike was going to happen, then this event was … . **unforeseeable**	If the purchaser is not happy with the performance of the supplier, then we can say that the purchaser is … **dissatisfied**

UNIT 3, Exercise 13 — File 06

Task 1
You are a lawyer. A client comes to you with a problem. He or she is going to give you a brief overview of the problem. Then you must ask questions to get all the necessary details. Try to use some of the language in the **useful phrases** box on page 35. Finally, give your client some advice about what to do.

Task 2

You are a client and you go to a lawyer with the following problem. Just give a brief overview of the problem. Then let the lawyer ask you questions to find out the details.

Overview

I asked a construction company to build a swimming pool for me in my garden. All of the specifications were agreed in the contract. The company has finished the work. But the pool which was built does not comply with the specifications we agreed to. I am not willing to pay the invoice of EUR 35,000. I think they should rebuild the pool.

Details

One of the specifications in the contract was that the deep end of the pool should measure 2.40 metres. This was to enable people to dive safely. When the pool was finished, it was clear that the deep end of the pool only measured 2.10 metres. Another problem was that the depth of the pool underneath the diving board was only 2 metres. I ordered a safety inspection. The inspector's report concluded that the pool was still safe for use. Nevertheless, I want the construction company to rebuild the pool to the specifications we originally agreed in our contract. The company says this would cost about EUR 30,000 and has offered me EUR 5,000 in compensation for my dissatisfaction. I would like to reject their offer because I don't see why I should accept something that isn't exactly what I wanted.

UNIT 4, Exercise 12 File 07

You are an attorney-at-law, acting on behalf of Mr. Billy Ratt (COMPOSER), a popular rap music artist. He is planning to enter into an exclusive copyright agreement with Global Music Inc. (PUBLISHER). The publisher has already sent you a draft version of the proposed agreement. However, you are unhappy with the following clauses:

1. COMPOSER … hereby undertakes to assign, transfer and deliver to PUBLISHER … the whole of the copyright for all countries of the world … in and to such music and lyrics written heretofore by COMPOSER insofar as such copyright is not held by third parties.
2. COMPOSER … will endeavour to deliver a minimum of ten compositions, each of which compromising three minutes of music on average, every year for the duration of this Agreement.
4. The rights of PUBLISHER include the right … to assign in whole or in part the compositions hereunder …
5. The term of the Agreement shall be for a period of three years from the date hereof. PUBLISHER shall have the option to renew this Agreement for a further period of three years.
8. PUBLISHER agrees to pay fees and royalties in respect of the compositions acquired hereunder to COMPOSER as follows:

   iii) 12.5 % of net receipts including the licensing of compositions for use in films, television programmes and commercials.
10. The royalty and fee statements shall be made up to June 30th and December 31st in each year and shall include all receipts by PUBLISHER in that period. Such statements will be sent to COMPOSER within 28 days of the relevant date and shall be accompanied by a remittance for the amounts which are shown by the statement to be due and payable.

Before you start the role-play, if possible, work with someone who has the same role and make sure you understand the reasons why you aren't happy with the draft clauses above.

During the role-play, try to get the best deal for your client.

Reasons

Clause 1 doesn't make it clear that the copyright reverts to the composer after the end of the agreement. You would like this to be clearly stated. Without such a statement, there is the risk that the publisher can retain the copyright for the duration of the copyright itself.

Clause 2 requires too much of the composer. You want a more flexible productivity commitment here.

Clause 4 gives the publisher assignment rights for any song by the composer. The composer wants more control over his material. He doesn't want his music used, for example, in commercials for products or services he doesn't agree with.

Clause 5 seems to suggest that the publisher can renew the agreement with or without the consent of the composer. Clarification is needed.

Clause 8 iii) is unfair. If the publisher allows the composer's music to be used in a movie, the composer has no material and production costs. The royalties should be much higher – for example, 80 %.

Clause 10 means the composer only receives payment twice a year. You want quarterly payments.

UNIT 5, Exercise 12 File 08

The company *Esskultur AG* is planning the acquisition of a UK company called *Fusion Food*.

You are a solicitor acting for *Fusion Food*. Here are some clauses from the draft version of the Letter of Intent. Have a meeting with the solicitor representing *Esskultur*. Your aim is to reach agreement with them about the precise wording of the LOI.

4 Exclusivity

(1) Beginning with the signing of this Letter of Intent until six months after the end of the due diligence period, the Seller shall not hold any discussions, either directly or indirectly, with any third party about the transfer of the Shares or of the Company's business operations. The Seller shall end any ongoing discussions.

(2) The exclusivity ends in any event upon the signature of the share purchase agreement or if one of the parties breaks off from the Transaction pursuant to 7(1).

(3) In the event the Seller breaches the exclusivity, it shall pay a contractual penalty in the amount of EUR 100,000 to the Purchaser. Further claims of the Purchaser shall remain unaffected. The contractual penalty shall not be payable, if binding contracts are concluded between the parties.

7 Binding Effect

(1) This Letter of Intent does not create any obligation to carry out the Transaction. Both parties shall be entitled to break off from the Transaction at any time before the share purchase agreement is signed, without having to give any reason. The notification of breaking-off must be in writing.

(2) The breaking-off shall not affect the applicability of the provisions in 4(3) and 7(3) of this Letter of Intent; these provisions shall remain binding.

(3) If the Seller breaks off the Transaction, it shall pay a lump-sum amount of EUR 100,000 to the Purchaser as compensation for its necessary expenses incurred in connection with the Transaction, unless the breaking-off is because of a breach by the Purchaser of the confidentiality obligation. If the Purchaser breaks off the Transaction, it shall pay a lump-sum amount of EUR 50,000 to the Seller as compensation for its necessary expenses, unless the breaking-off is because of a breach by the Seller of the exclusivity or confidentiality obligations. More extensive claims resulting from the breaking-off of the Transaction shall remain unaffected.

Your position

4.1 is a problem. You can accept that *Fusion Food* should not start talks with a third party. You can't accept that it should break off any ongoing discussions with third parties. If *Fusion Food* has the freedom to continue ongoing discussions with a third party, then it can put *Esskultur* under pressure if the third party is offering better terms.

This penalty is too high. A fairer and more realistic sum would be: EUR 50,000 if *Esskultur AG* has completed due diligence and EUR 25,000 if due diligence is still in progress.

You are against the idea that *Esskultur AG* should have the right to make further claims against your client. The penalty agreed in clause 4.3 must be sufficient. If *Esskultur AG* has the right to make further claims, then you could get into a long-running legal dispute, which would not be in your client's interests. *Esskultur AG* also needs an incentive (*Anreiz*) to keep its costs under control.

The penalty in clause 7.3 should be the same as in clause 4.3. You don't think the compensation for *Fusion Food* should be lower than the compensation for *Esskultur AG*. After all, the purchaser should take its obligations seriously, too.

Follow up

Present to the class any changes you have agreed to make to the wording of the Letter of Intent.

UNIT 6, Exercise 3 File 09

1 Your partner is going to read out some sentences to you. Listen and try to provide the missing word.

2 Read out the sentences below but don't read out the phrasal verb in bold in parenthese. See if your partner can find the word you are looking for.

- I think we can help you to **BLANK** bankruptcy, but the company will have to go into administration. (**ward off**)
- It is my understanding that, if you implement a radical cost-cutting programme, your creditors will be willing to **BLANK** you **BLANK**. (**bale out**)
- I strongly advise you to change your company's tax status. If you don't do something to reduce your tax burden, your company could **BLANK**. (**go under**)
- I recommend that you formally object to this latest tax demand. Paying this sum by the end of next month could **BLANK** you **BLANK** completely. (**wipe out**)

UNIT 6, Exercise 11 File 10

You are Ranjit Singh. You are going to meet with an insolvency lawyer. You have already sent him/her the following brief overview of your assets and liabilities. All the sums of money are in euros.

Liabilities		*Assets*	
Banks		*Flat*	*110,000*
Bank loan	*25,000*	*Receivables (unpaid invoices for party service and events)*	*8,000*
Mortgage (on flat)	*85,000*	*Inventory (kitchen equipment/ furniture)*	*10,000*
Staff			
Part-time employees	*6,000*		
Other creditors			
Utilities	*2,500*		
Landlord of premises	*6,500*		
Suppliers of fresh food	*2,500*		
Telephone/Internet	*500*		
Tax authorities	*18,000*		
Total	*146,000*	*Total*	*128,000*

Your lawyer has told you that he/she will want to know a lot more about your business and financial situation, so you have decided to take these notes along to your first meeting.

I worked for many years as a food technologist for a large supermarket chain. Four years ago I got married to Sabine – she was a student at Nottingham University at the time – and moved from Nottingham to ______________________________ (agree a town with your partner). Sabine is a full-time parent at home looking after our children.

At first I found work in an event-catering company. Then I sold my flat in England and used some of the profit from the sale to make a down payment on a flat here in ______________________________. The flat cost EUR140,000 and is in my name. The mortgage was just EUR90,000.

Two years I decided to go into business as a sole trader providing fresh Indian snacks and event catering for office workers and companies. I rented some business premises in a smart canal-side office development. The start-up costs for the business were EUR45,000: EUR10,000 of this sum was my own capital and EUR35,000 was a bank loan secured against my flat.

Business went well for a while, but recently there has been a dramatic economic downturn. The lunchtime trade has fallen away and I can no longer cover my costs. A business rescue plan seems pointless because the surrounding office buildings continue to lose tenants.

Over the last two years I have kept up with my mortgage and loan repayments, but during this time the flat has fallen in value by EUR30,000.

Your lawyer will give you advice about what to do. Ask about anything that isn't clear.
Listen to your lawyer present the advice he gave you. Then tell the class whether you intend to follow it.

Transcripts

2 **UNIT 1, EXERCISE 3 — Part 1**

Anke Nice to see you again, Mr. Osborne. Business is good, I trust.

Matthew Not bad, not bad. Some ups and downs but I can't complain.

Anke Now, you mentioned on the phone that you wanted to consult me on the question of forming a new company or perhaps changing the structure of your existing company. How exactly can I help you?

Matthew Well, I'm thinking of getting into something new with my property business and I'd like to discuss the legal implications with you.

Anke Up till now you've dealt exclusively with commercial property, haven't you?

Matthew That's right. Some of the office buildings I acquired have been resold and some are let. But I'm thinking of moving into the holiday apartment sector. I feel that the growth potential there is greater than in the commercial sector.

Anke I can't see any problems here for your GmbH. Or are you thinking of forming a separate company specialising in holiday apartments?

Matthew No, that hadn't crossed my mind. I am thinking of offering my finance and marketing directors the chance to come in as shareholders, but that's a fairly straightforward business, isn't it?

Anke Absolutely. All these options are covered in the articles of association we drew up five years ago. We can very easily bring in your two directors as shareholders.

Matthew Fine.

Anke And concerning the planned change of focus of your company, we can change the objects clause in your memorandum of association to include holiday apartment development and management. It's a relatively simple procedure.

Matthew Of course, we're going to have to do that anyway. But I have a new concept for developing and letting holiday apartments and this is where I need your advice.

3 **UNIT 1, EXERCISE 3 — Part 2**

Matthew Let me explain. You see, my company's market research tells me that up on the Baltic coast the growing demand for holiday accommodation can no longer be met by the traditional resorts like Bansin, Heringsdorf or Ahlbeck. So new, less fashionable resorts like Karlshagen have to be developed. The problem is that investors are nervous. They are often worried that their property will stand empty for a great number of weeks during the year. So my idea is to bundle all the different owners in one apartment building and to offer each of them a minimum guaranteed rental income for the year.

Anke I'm not sure I would recommend doing that. If some apartments in a building stand empty, that's simply going to cost you money. Isn't this an enormous risk?

Matthew Yes and no. I think that my company is pretty good at assessing risk in the property sector. What's more, the guaranteed minimum annual rent will be a little lower than the market rent that I think is achievable.

Anke So, if all the apartments are let, you earn the difference between the minimum guaranteed rent and the actual rent.

Matthew I don't take all the difference. I take 25% of it – as a kind of performance bonus, if you like. In addition, I make a very modest charge – let's say 20 or 25 cents per m^2 per month for administering the whole thing.

Anke But what's in it for the investors?

Matthew Firstly, the investor is investing with minimum risk because he has a guaranteed minimum annual income. Secondly, if the apartments are let successfully and at market rents, the investor receives 75% of any income above the minimum which I have guaranteed.

Anke I see. So, if one apartment stands empty for large parts of the holiday season, you will be able to finance the minimum rent from the rental income from all the other apartments in the property.

Matthew Exactly.

Anke And if one-third of the apartments stand empty for long periods of time? What then?

Matthew Then my company would have to pay the minimum annual rent from its own funds until it succeeded in letting the empty apartments more successfully.

Anke That's the risk I was worried about.

Matthew But I don't think it would come to that.

Anke Nevertheless, I don't think you should allow yourself to be liable for unlimited sums. I suggest doing something to limit your liability here.

Matthew Sounds like very good advice.

Anke But can I just come back to the investors? In a way, they are cross-subsidising each other in order to guarantee a minimum rental income for all the apartments in the property.

Matthew Exactly.

Anke Then the investors would have to be in some kind of legal structure. I mean, you can't run this idea by simply having a separate contract with each investor.

Matthew That's exactly my point and that's why I've come to see you.

4 **UNIT 2, EXERCISE 3**

Torsten ... the 1st of January. Fine. So, I'll put that starting date into your contract. Before we finish, Mrs. O'Brien, you mentioned on the phone last Friday that there are a few things in your contract you'd like to discuss before signing it.

Cathy Well, yes. There are just a few points that I'd like to clarify with you.

Torsten No problem. What would you like to know?

Cathy Well, in clause 1, paragraph 2, it says that the

normal working time will be 38 hours a week. But it doesn't say anywhere that the normal working week is Monday to Friday.

Torsten Well, usually it is, but occasionally our software people have to come in at the weekend if there's an important deadline to meet or some other difficulty. So, I think that's why the wording is as it is.

Cathy Wouldn't it be possible to add something to that effect? For example, the normal working week is Monday to Friday but sometimes it will be necessary ... Something like that?

Torsten I'm sure that'll be OK.

Cathy Fine. And then I've got a question about annual leave. Err ... Yes, here it is. According to clause 6, if I can't take all my holiday, I can have financial compensation for up to 15 days of it.

Torsten Yes, that's right. If there is a lot of work and you aren't able to take your full leave entitlement, we don't want you to lose out. That's the reason for this particular clause.

Cathy I understand. But if this happens, can't I carry 15 days' holiday into the next working year?

Torsten I suppose, in theory you could. We've just never really felt it was necessary to write it down. And, in any case, employees are usually quite happy to receive the extra pay if they can't take some of their holiday. Another problem, of course, is that in the following year someone might be entitled to 30 days' plus 15 days' annual leave. That's a lot of holiday!

Cathy Well, as you know from my job interview, I have a young family and I really would prefer to have something in my contract that guarantees me my full holiday entitlement. Even if it means carrying leave into the following year.

Torsten Mmm ... I'd like to check this with our lawyer. I can't imagine that there would be any legal difficulties here; it's more a question of company policy with respect to senior staff. Let me get back to you on that one. I don't want to make any promises at this stage but I'm sure we'll be able to find some kind of compromise on this.

Cathy OK ... And there's just one more thing. It's clause 4, paragraph 5. It says that ... "There is no claim to compensation for overtime, weekend or holiday work."

Torsten Yes, that's quite standard for senior staff contracts. Of course, in the case of employees who are earning standard union pay rates we have to pay overtime or give the employees the time back.

Cathy I see. But, as a senior staff member I wouldn't be entitled to any pay for overtime.

Torsten That's right.

Cathy But does it also mean that I wouldn't be entitled to have any of this time back, either?

Torsten Not necessarily. I think you'll find that senior staff usually sort something out with their line managers. It all depends on how much work there is at any one time.

Cathy I see. I'm just wondering if all this could be stated a bit more clearly in the contract. Can't we add a paragraph that says something like ... er ... "Overtime may be taken as free time. But this must be with the agreement of the line manager."? Or something like that?

Torsten I'm assuming there won't be any legal complications here. But, again, I'll have to check with our lawyer on this.

Cathy OK. That's everything. The rest of the contract seems to be fine.

Torsten Good. I'll send all this off to the lawyer and I'll mail you in the next day or two to let you know what he thinks.

Cathy Great. I'll expect to hear from you soon, then. And thank you for taking the time to discuss all these things with me. I'll get back to my flat hunting now.

Torsten Well, good luck with that. If you run into any difficulties, do let me know. The company would be able to organise some accommodation for you for two or three months, if necessary.

Cathy I'll certainly bear your offer in mind, Mr. Schwarz. Thank you once again for your time. Bye.

UNIT 2, EXERCISE 10

5

Mary ... the matter of Mrs. O'Brien's resignation. Now, I've had a look at all the documents you sent me, Mr. Flannagan and ... well the first thing I've noticed is Mrs. O'Brien's actual letter of resignation. You see, according to her contract, she isn't entitled to start her new job as early as the 1st of January – unless, of course, you're happy to let her go early.

John Yes, I'd noticed that, too. But that isn't really what I'm worried about. My biggest concern is that the company she's planning to go to is Softline in Germany.

Mary Yes, I wanted to come to that. Looking at your files, I can see that Softline has become an important cooperation partner for your company.

John Exactly.

Mary Well, if Softline has started to poach your staff, it's very irritating, I admit. But, in reality, there isn't very much you can do about it.

John Actually, I'm worried about confidentiality.

Mary I see. Well, you can, of course, invoke clause 7.6 of Mrs. O'Brien's contract, which says, quite simply, that you can send her home today on gardening leave. The only problem there is that you would have to continue to pay her for the full period of her notice – that is ... er ... three months' salary. Quite a lot of money. But it may be worth it.

John What about the competition clause? You know – the one that says that the employee isn't allowed to go and work for a competitor for two years.

Mary Well that would be difficult. You see, we can hardly say that Softline is a competitor, when you have cooperation agreements with them. The other problem is that the competition clause would be very expensive for you as a company. Clause 3.4 states that you would have to pay Mrs. O'Brien half-pay for two years – and she wouldn't have to do any work for this money.

John It would cost us a lot more money if we lost know-how to a competitor. Anyway, there's a further complication. You see, we aren't Softline's only cooperation partner in the field of telecommunications software development. And some of Softline's other partners are direct competitors of ours.

Mary Mm. And what exactly will Mrs. O'Brien's new job be at Softline?

John To coordinate all their external software development projects.
Mary So there is a risk that your company's know-how might be transferred to a competitor.
John Indeed there is. So, can't I invoke clause ... er ... 3.2? It says here quite clearly that ... the employee can't work for a competitor or – I quote – "a firm connected with them." I mean, I can stop her, can't I?
Mary Perhaps. But I wouldn't want you to overreact to what may be only a very small risk. And another thing. If you do anything to delay Mrs. O'Brien's transfer to Softline, they're not going to be very pleased with you. This could even have a negative impact on future cooperation agreements.
John So, what do you suggest I do?
Mary To be honest, I think it would be best to ...

6

UNIT 3, EXERCISE 5

1 Just a question about the penalty clause. Can we reduce the price by 1% if Pixeltechnik delivers four days late?
2 Where exactly does it say in this contract how many items we have to order?
3 Where can we find all the prices for the different LCD screens?
4 I'm just looking at clause 4. Can Pixeltechnik increase the price if it wants to?
5 I'm a little unclear about clause 5. Is this a two-year contract?
6 What exactly are our rights if Pixeltechnik goes bankrupt?
7 There's something in clause 10 I'd like to clarify. What happens if some goods are defective? Can we insist on a replacement?
8 What happens if another company suddenly claims that it owns the patent on Pixeltechnik's LCD screen technology? Can we be sued by this company?

7

UNIT 3, EXERCISE 9 Part 1

Herr Hörner ... and it was very good of you to fit me in at such short notice.
Mr. Evans Not at all, Mr. Hörner. I think the quicker we can work out a response to this matter the better. Now, let me see. I have here a copy of the original contract between Pixeltechnik and Digital View and I also have a copy of the correspondence which was exchanged between the two companies. But can I start by asking you to describe what happened?
Herr Hörner Well, in September I was contacted by my production manager. He informed me that our random sampling was showing inconsistencies in every single LCD screen and that he was going to shut production down.
Mr. Evans And what happened then?
Herr Hörner I joined him in the production area and we organised a series of checks to find out what the problem was. It turned out to be a minor error in chemical processing. It meant that the screens were not consistently as bright as they should have been.
Mr. Evans Could you explain what you mean by "not consistently"?
Herr Hörner Well, the screens might still have conformed to the agreed product specifications, but they didn't pass our stringent testing regime. And that's what matters. You see, the whole process is patented. It means that our digital camera display screens can be seen perfectly – even in bright sunshine and ...
Mr. Evans Yes, but let me take you back to the question of these defects. Are you saying that the screens were not defective as defined in Annex 1 to the contract?
Herr Hörner I think as far as the contractual specifications are concerned the screens were probably still OK. But we knew there was a processing error. The screens might have developed malfunctions at a later stage. We just thought it was best for the reputation of Pixeltechnik not to take any risks.
Mr. Evans OK. Can you explain why you had to recall so many screens? 5,000 wasn't it?
Herr Hörner At first, we thought that one batch – 500 – was affected. But when we checked the sample data it became clear that we had had the error for about ten days.
Mr. Evans So, if I understand you correctly, you're saying that your production manager only found the production error ten days after it started.
Herr Hörner I'm afraid that's right. For ten days the test results showed slight inconsistencies in screen brightness but it seems that our technicians misinterpreted the results and thought the screens were fine.

8

UNIT 3, EXERCISE 9 Part 2

Mr. Evans What did your company do then?
Herr Hörner We contacted Digital View immediately and informed them about the product recall.
Mr. Evans And how did they react?
Herr Hörner They weren't very pleased, but we agreed on a schedule for delivery of 5,000 LCD screens and Pixeltechnik accepted the full financial consequences of late delivery.
Mr. Evans This would be clause 1.4 ... er ... "... for every week or part thereof by which the delivery date is exceeded, the purchaser can reduce the agreed price for the order by 2%."
Herr Hörner Quite a lot of money, I might add.
Mr. Evans Have you calculated precisely how much?
Herr Hörner I haven't got the exact figures from our Finance Manager yet, but it's somewhere in the region of 15,000 euros.
Mr. Evans So, reasonable compensation for any inconvenience suffered by Digital View, one would think.
Herr Hörner Indeed.
Mr. Evans Did you deliver the 5,000 screens according to the agreed schedule?
Herr Hörner Yes, we did. And the product quality was 100% as well. That's why I was so shocked to receive this letter yesterday. I mean they can't just terminate the contract with 21 days' notice, can they? Surely this is breach of contract!
Mr. Evans Well, they are invoking clause 8.1(i), which refers to unsatisfactory performance. That could be a slight problem for us. Was this the first time you had had quality problems?
Herr Hörner Yes, it was. So, in my view, it's completely unfair. We did a lot of extra development work on our product – just for Digital View – and we won't

begin to make a profit on this deal until after two years of production. So if we get thrown out of this contract now, we'll suffer an enormous loss.

Mr. Evans I suppose that's why the contract was to run for a minimum of two years.

Herr Hörner Exactly. And our patented product really gave Digital View the edge over its competitors.

Mr. Evans I must say, it does seem unfair. It's possible that Digital View could be using this production problem as an excuse to get out of a contract that it no longer wants for strategic reasons.

Herr Hörner But is there anything we can do about it?

Mr. Evans Well, as I see it, Digital View's conduct goes against the whole spirit of your agreement. In view of this, our best option would be to ...

9

UNIT 4, EXERCISE 9

William Good morning to you in New York. I'd like to start by confirming who is present at this video conference. My name is William Field and I'm acting on behalf of my client Mr. Fabian Stein, the Chief Executive of the Berlin-based film company, Linke Hand Produktion.

Fiona And I'm Fiona Martinez, attorney-at-law, acting on behalf of my client, Jake Glover, who is the Financial Director of Index Films here in New York.

William So. We are all in possession of the draft version of the proposed agreement. Could I suggest that we hand over to Mr. Stein and Mr. Glover?

Jake Maybe we could start by agreeing on a sum of money here. What kind of figure did you have in mind, Mr. Stein?

Fabian Well, I was thinking of an initial down payment followed by a later payment after the release of the film. The total would be in the region of 60,000 euros.

Jake I'm afraid my board might find that figure rather low. After all, you are asking us to waive our right to exclusivity here.

Fabian I appreciate that, Mr. Glover. But this is a low-budget film. If we agreed to a significantly higher sum, the project could quickly cease to be viable.

Jake Well, we might be able to agree to your figure if we could participate in the film's royalties.

Fabian I don't think that will be possible. But perhaps you could accept a figure of, say, a maximum of 75,000 euros, depending on the success of the film.

Jake You mean, if your movie flops, we would get nothing.

Fabian Not quite. You would still have the down payment.

Jake And how much did you have in mind?

Fabian I think 20,000 euros would be fair.

Jake Let me see if I understand you here. Index Films would get a guaranteed payment of 20,000 euros. Any further payment would be limited to the balance, namely 55,000 euros, and if the film flopped, we'd get zilch.

Fabian Well, yes. But that's putting it rather negatively. I'm simply trying to suggest a framework which would give you some kind of share in the success of the film.

Jake Now that I think about it, maybe a success-related payment would only lead to endless arguments between lawyers and accountants. Why not drop the idea and have a 40,000 euros down payment and 50,000 euros within one year of the release of your movie?

Fabian I could agree to the 40,000 euros down payment if we reduced the second payment to 30,000 euros.

Jake 30,000 euros isn't really high enough. I could compromise on 45,000 euros but on the condition that we clarify the terms for the down payment.

Fabian Mm. The down payment would be conditional upon our securing the formal agreement of the publishers.

William And we do already have a signed Letter of Intent from the publishers in this matter.

Fiona But letters of intent are, as you know, just that. They aren't necessarily legally binding. Your negotiations with the publisher could drag on for months and months and during all this time my client's hands would be tied. No payment and no freedom to negotiate with other third parties.

William How about setting a time limit for the down payment? Let's say six months following the signing of our agreement, or the deal is off.

Jake Well, in view of what you just said about your Letter of Intent, I'd have thought that six months was a little too long. How about three months?

Fabian I think I could agree to that.

Jake So, to summarise. You would make an initial down payment of 40,000 euros within three months...

Fabian Not payable, of course, if we get a rejection from the publishers.

Jake Sure. And you would pay a further 45,000 euros within one year of the movie's release.

Fabian I think 45,000 euros is a little high. However, I could agree to 35,000 euros.

Jake And I think my board would be happier with 40,000 euros.

Fabian Agreed.

William Fine. I'll draw up a final agreement ready for signature and will notify you as soon as we have secured the agreement of the publishers in this matter. Thank you very much for your time, Mr. Glover and Ms. Martinez and ...

10

UNIT 5, EXERCISE 2

Regina You have reached the office of Regina Möller. I am unable to take your call at the moment. Please leave a message after the tone.

Matt Hi there, Regina. It's Matt. I just had a look through our company's M&A documentation and I'm sort of confused. Some of it's in German; some of it's in English and one or two things seem to be – I dunno – some kind of post-merger documents. Do you think you could get all this into some kind of shape for me? What I'd like is a straightforward guide to the steps we have to take when trying to make an acquisition up to the point when the whole thing enters the public domain. And I guess I need to know where all those minefields are, too. Can you do that for me, Regina? Thanks a lot. Talk to you later.

UNIT 5, EXERCISE 9 Part 1

11

Matt Hi Regina. Hi Oliver. OK. I know you've both got full schedules right now, so let's get started. Now, our solicitors in the UK have completed the due diligence process on our target company, "No Frills". Can you take us through their findings, Regina?

Regina Certainly. Well, what you have in front of you is a summary prepared by Stefan, our trainee lawyer. You can inspect the original documents in my office at any time, of course. And ... no unpleasant surprises really. It's a limited company, registered in England since 2005 and ... is still owned by its three original founders. It's grown to 16 retro-style English cafés – seems to have good growth prospects. The finances are sound. There's £300,000 of fully paid-up equity and all growth has been organic.

Oliver I'm sorry, Regina. What do you mean by "organic"?

Regina Er ... I mean that the growth has financed itself. The company hasn't borrowed in order to finance expansion. So, as far as we can tell, the company has no debts and there are no charges against it.

Matt And what about their public health clearance certificates, disabled access to restroom facilities, staff qualifications – all that kind of thing?

Regina No problems there, either. It almost seems to be too good to be true but ...

Oliver Sorry to butt in, Regina but what's your opinion of the current leases for many of the café premises? According to these findings, the company has generally gone for very short leases. Isn't it a bit over exposed?

Regina I'm sorry, Oliver. I'm not quite with you.

Oliver I mean, when leases expire, there's often the risk that the landlord wants to negotiate a much higher rent.

Regina I see. Well, yes. In principle, that's true but it doesn't seem to be a risk that the solicitors chose to highlight.

Matt Maybe not, but I think Oliver's got a point here. Surely something like this is quantifiable, isn't it? What's your opinion, Oliver?

Oliver I think it is, yes. I mean, I'm sure Regina is right. But it would be nice to know what potential additional operating costs the company might be facing.

Regina No, I agree. Better to be safe than sorry. I can ask the solicitors to go through all the leasehold agreements again and to check commercial rents in all the relevant locations. Then Oliver and I can have a short meeting to re-assess the level of risk.

Matt And when do you think you'll be able to give me the figures?

Regina Err ... It depends on our solicitors. I mean, it's one or two days' work at most. So we could ask them to get back to us by Thursday. Oliver? Would you have time for a meeting on Friday?

Oliver Sure. I've got appointments through most of the afternoon but the morning's free. Shall we say 9.30 and then we can get our figures to Matt by lunchtime?

Regina Sounds fine.

Matt Good. Now before we move on I'd just like to say one more thing ...

UNIT 5, EXERCISE 9 Part 2

12

Matt So, we can't yet confirm our offer price but, assuming it would be in the region of £7.5 million, what are our financing options?

Oliver Basically, there are three options – some of which could be combined. We can finance the acquisition out of our capital reserves, we can borrow, or we can pay the three current owners in the form of newly issued shares in Esskultur AG.

Matt And which option do you favour, Oliver?

Oliver I'd prefer to issue new shares to the value of £7.5 million and buy out the owners that way. The limited company continues to exist as before. There's just a change of owner, that's all. Esskultur AG would be entered into the Register of Companies as the owner of 100% of the equity of "No Frills".

Matt Any views on that, Regina?

Regina Well, it's perfectly possible, of course. But there's always the risk of upsetting existing shareholders. We have some quite important institutional shareholders and they might worry about the impact of a new share issue on their own shareholding. And we shouldn't forget – company law stipulates that the shareholders have the right to buy newly issued shares. We would need to get a 75% vote from them in favour of waiving their right to these shares before we could offer them to the three owners of "No Frills". Votes like this can be risky.

Matt And bringing in loan capital?

Oliver and Regina I'm against it / I'm not in favour. You see, borrowing conditions are not so easy at the moment, so we might be looking at fairly unattractive rates of interest and a drain on the company's finances for the entire repayment period.

Matt And what about taking the money out of capital reserves? I reckon we need the shareholders' approval here, Regina.

Regina Absolutely. It's needed for any acquisition of a company or a stake in a company involving an obligation of more than 2 million euros. But we would avoid the complications of a share issue.

Oliver Of course, you're right, Regina. But our capital reserves amount to 10 million euros at the moment. I don't want them to become so depleted that we over-expose ourselves. After all, our recent acquisition "The Bread Company" isn't doing so well and we may have to ask the shareholders to approve a release of capital from our reserves to finance investment there.

Matt Yeah, it's as I thought. There's no easy answer here but I think we're all agreed that "No Frills" represents an excellent acquisition opportunity. So why don't we now ...?

UNIT 6, EXERCISE 5

13

Jana You have reached Jana Burzinski. I'm afraid I'm not available to take your call right now. But if you leave your name and number, I'll get back to you as soon as possible.

Piet Hi Jana. Piet Forster here. I got your e-mail. Glad that everything checked out OK. On the risk audit issue – yeah – I see where you're coming from on this. As you say, it could be very important, so I – er – don't have a problem with paying for legal services if all this is really going to get us somewhere. To come back to your e-mail – you don't really go into any detail about the scope of the audit you have in mind. So – er – before you go ahead, can you fill me in on that? Thanks. Speak to you soon. Bye.

14

UNIT 6, EXERCISE 7

Piet So, let's move on to the main reason for our meeting today – this risk assessment analysis you've both been working on. Jana, how do you want to proceed on this?

Jana Well, I thought it would be interesting to hear from Florian first and then I can go on to set out some of the other risks we might be facing.

Piet Fine. So, Florian. How do things look from your point of view?

Florian Generally good. But I did find clauses in three agreements that we should perhaps look at in more detail. I've – uh – prepared a print out of the relevant clauses and I will try to keep things as straightforward as possible.

Piet Well, I'm certainly grateful for that, Florian.

Florian Now the first document I'd like to draw your attention to is the leasehold agreement for our offices here in Vienna.

Piet It's coming up for renewal soon, isn't it?

Florian Exactly. As you can see from clause 2.6, the lease is automatically extended by five years unless we specifically state in writing twelve months before the termination date that we don't want this.

Piet But where's the problem?

Florian I think it's clause 5 that's the problem. You see, your rent for these premises has been rising steadily over the past five years in line with the consumer price index whereas typical rents for commercial and office space in this part of the city have been falling. Basically, you're probably paying about 10 to 15% too much at the moment. What's more, if this agreement is automatically extended, then clause 5 will continue to apply for the next term of five years.

Piet I see. So what do you suggest we do?

Florian Under no circumstances should you just allow the lease to be extended automatically. I suggest you state in writing as soon as possible that you waive your right under clause 2.6 but that you wish to negotiate a new lease for these premises. This will give you the chance to renegotiate clause 5 and thus save quite a lot of money. You are also holding an option on 200 m² of office space on the 2nd floor. Do you really need that space? I mean, you haven't needed it so far. If you renegotiate, you can get that clause removed.

Piet OK. That all makes sense. And the other things you noticed?

Florian Well, I had a look at the redundancy clause in your works council agreement and I think it would be better to renegotiate the size of the compensation you're offering in case of redundancy. I mean, three months' salary for every year's service could be very expensive if you had to lay off 15 or 20 staff one day. I think, too, that the compensation clause should specifically state that such a payment would be gross and subject to all the relevant deductions – social insurance, tax etc.

Piet So this three months thing isn't some statutory amount.

Florian No, not at all. This is an entirely voluntary arrangement and one that is potentially disadvantageous to you.

Piet Fine. I can ask the HR manager to get onto that. And you found one more thing too, didn't you?

Florian Yes. It's a clause agreed with Finnwood, the Finnish timber processors you acquired at the end of last year.

Piet But that whole acquisition has been a great success so far!

Florian Absolutely. It's just that ...

Jana Maybe I could just come in here.

Florian Sure, by all means.

Jana You see, when we acquired Finnwood, valuing the company was not at all easy. So, we inserted this price adjustment clause. It's all about the company's liquidity and, essentially, it means that we may have to pay a little extra at the beginning of next year.

Piet How much?

Jana It depends on some quite complex calculations, but it could be as high as 500,000 euros.

Piet Are you suggesting that we challenge this agreement?

Florian Not at all. The agreement is quite fair and reasonable. What I would recommend is that, at the beginning of next year when you decide on profit allocation in the company, you allocate an appropriate sum to the capital reserves in order to cover this risk.

Piet Is that going to be possible, Jana?

Jana Definitely. It's just going to mean less money going to the shareholders next year or being available for investment.

Piet I can see that there's more to this risk management business than I realized. Before we discuss Jana's findings, why don't we take a short break and ...

15

UNIT 6, EXERCISE 10

Piet Thank you both for coming at such short notice. As you've probably seen in the financial press this morning, one of our major clients, Fuller's Construction Ltd. in the UK, has gone bankrupt. I've called this meeting to find out exactly what this means for us. Maybe you could fill us in on the legal side of things, Florian.

Florian Certainly. Well, I've checked the Register of Companies and Fuller's Construction is listed there as being in compulsory liquidation.

Piet Sounds bad.

Florian I'm afraid it does. You see, the directors of the company clearly took the view that the company couldn't service its debts and couldn't be rescued. They could have filed for an administration order but they didn't – instead they petitioned the court to make a winding-up order.

Piet I'm afraid you've lost me, Florian.

Jana Me too.

Florian Sorry. Basically, when a company is "in administration" then the administrator is trying to keep as much of the company going as possible. But when a court issues a winding-up order, it appoints a liquidator whose job it is to realize the assets of the company in order to satisfy its creditors.

Piet I see. So the whole company is going to be sold off.

Florian Well, its assets, yes.

Piet And how do we stand with Fuller's Construction right now, Jana?
Jana It's not looking too good, I'm afraid. They defaulted on payment on one very large order six months ago. Then they made another large order and we restructured the whole terms of payment. I checked our records just a few minutes ago. They were due to pay the first instalment at the beginning of last month but ...
Piet So how much are we owed?
Jana About 1.5 million euros, I'm afraid.
Piet *(sounding resigned)* Well, I suppose we will just have to register ourselves as a creditor and wait to get back – well – some of what we're owed at least.
Florian I'm not sure we can count on that.
Piet You're going to have to explain that.
Florian Basically, Form and Function is a supplier and qualifies as an unsecured creditor. Ahead of you are preferential creditors like the employees, who may be owed wages and secured creditors or charge holders like banks, who lent money to the company and secured the loan against the company's assets. And then there are the costs of the liquidation process itself. They too have to be paid before the unsecured creditors can be satisfied.
Piet So what would you advise?
Florian Well, certainly you should register as a creditor. But, if I remember the sale of goods contract for this client, title doesn't pass to the buyer until the goods have been paid for. It could be possible to get the goods back again.
Piet Jana?
Jana I'm not sure we would really benefit. I mean some of the furniture is already in use. Another problem is that it was custom-built to the specifications of the client. We might be able to offload it for a few hundred thousand euros. But there's the damage to our brand to consider if we start selling second-hand goods at knock-down prices.
Piet So the worst case scenario is that we will have to take a hit of 1.5 million euros. Can we do that?
Jana Well, I've been going through the figures and I imagine that, with some debt restructuring, with some cost cuts across all levels of the company and possibly with voluntary redundancies of 20 or 30 staff, we'll be able to get through this with our core business intact.
Piet Sounds too good to be true. Maybe you could go through the figures and then ...

Answer key

UNIT 1

page 5

Preamble

Unlimited liability
This problem exists for self-employed people and for ordinary partnerships (*Personengesellschaften*). In these cases the business is not a separate legal entity. This means that liability rests with the owner(s) of the company. If the company has debts, the owner is liable for them and is not allowed to limit this liability – even if it means him losing the roof over his head. In a corporation (*Kapitalgesellschaft*) the liability of a shareholder is limited to the value of the shares he or she holds.

Articles of association / articles of incorporation
– see Info Box below letter on page 10

Equity / Company capital
The law says that for limited companies a certain amount of cash or assets must be paid in when the company is formed. The law does not require a minimum amount of equity for partnerships. This company capital must always be available so that there are at least some assets left to satisfy creditors if the company goes bankrupt.

Tangible assets
"Assets" is another word for property. There are different categories of assets, and tangible assets are physical objects e.g. equipment, buildings, vehicles, raw materials. Intangible assets are not physical objects but they have a value e.g. goodwill, know-how, patents.

Freelancer
Freelancers are self-employed people who are members of certain professions e.g. journalism, teaching, architecture, accountancy, design. If you do not exercise a freelance occupation, you are a sole-trader and must register with the trade office and possibly the craftsmen's guild, too.

Commercial register
Many partnerships and all corporations must be entered in the commercial register. This register contains key information about the company e.g. the name of the company and the address of its head office, the names of its directors, the date of its formation, the kind of business it conducts and the size of its share capital. This information can be inspected by any member of the public and is increasingly available on the Internet.

1
1 on your own
2 debts
3 personal
4 agreement
5 owners
6 separate
7 shareholding
8 cash
9 publicly
10 profits

page 7

2
Limited liability partnerships are indeed becoming more popular amongst lawyers, accountants and architects, whose liability can run to millions of euros. The German *Partnerschaft* does not limit personal liability but there is no longer liability for other partners in the partnership.

This is a balance that the lawmaker must strike. High mandatory levels of equity create confidence in a company but make life difficult for entrepreneurs. Low mandatory levels of equity – as in the case of the English limited company – are good news for entrepreneurs but make life more risky for creditors.

The distinction between trades and freelance professions has its roots in history. One thing that is common to freelance professions is that the relationship of freelancers with clients is characterized by a particular confidentiality. What is, however, a disadvantage for many freelance professions is that the occupation title e.g. teacher, translator, consultant is not legally protected. This is not true of occupations like plumber, glazier or carpenter.

This is a particular problem for young companies but one has to have some understanding for a bank in this situation. Life gets easier once a company is established. Then its directors might secure new bank loans against the company's assets, not their personal assets.

3 Part 1
1 He buys and sells and also lets commercial property.
2 He would like to bring them in as shareholders.
3 five years ago
4 holiday apartment lettings
5 The growth potential in the holiday apartment sector is greater.

page 8

3 Part 2
a the market rent.
b 20
c 25
d 25
e rental income from the other apartments in the property
f the client's company.
g limit his liability
h separate contract with each owner

page 9

5
1 c
2 f
3 a
4 d
5 b
6 e

page 10

6 2 Yes. Osborne Real Estate could buy a small apartment in each property and then the company could be the managing partner of the GbR with Matthew as its representative.
3 Not necessarily. If the partnership agreement is drawn up tightly enough and the relationship between Matthew's company as managing agent and the GbR is set out in detail, Matthew doesn't need his company to be part of the GbR.
4 Yes. The duration of the partnership and the way in which it can be terminated. Matthew might not make a loss but he might find that he isn't making any profit either. In this situation, he might want to get out of this legal relationship with the GbR.

7 1 g
2 e
3 i
4 j
5 a
6 b
7 c
8 h
9 f
10 d

8 1 view / the commercial register
2 issuing / shares
3 obtained / a certificate of incorporation
4 conduct / business
5 reject / an application
6 draw up / a partnership agreement
7 raise / capital
8 debts / incur

page 12

9 1 b
2 c
3 d
4 f
5 a
6 e

page 13

11 1 First of all
2 Then
3 Following that
4 last of all
5 At first
6 Firstly
7 secondly
8 finally

12 (suggested answer)
- Creditors have little or no security during the first few years of the *mini-GmbH's* existence.
- The requirement of 25,000 euros equity is a way of making sure that entrepreneurs don't go into business lightly – taking risks at the expense of their clients and creditors.
- If mini-GmbHs get a bad reputation, this could damage the image of the GmbH too.
- It is not clear what will happen if a *mini-GmbH* doesn't build up enough equity quickly to convert to a full GmbH. Can it continue trading or must it cease trading?

page 14

13 a 3
b 5
c 6
d 8
e 4
f 10
g 9
h 2
i 7
j 1

14 a There are some very large companies in Germany that have remained private limited companies e.g. Merck and Bosch.

Advantages
- The company is protected from hostile takeover bids.
- The shareholders are often primarily members of an extended family and will always act to preserve the integrity and continuity of the company.
- The company is free of the obligations that would be imposed on a large plc, e.g. mandatory quarterly reports.

Disadvantages
- The company has less access to capital – a possible problem if it wanted to embark on a major investment programme.
- Family in-fighting can make decisions more difficult.
- Company less willing to bring in outside expertise to freshen up its performance.

b This is not uncommon in situations where it is very important to move fast.

Advantages
- The company is already registered so the amount of time needed before you can commence trading is very short.
- Time might be very important. Imagine a situation in which you want to manufacture and distribute spin-off articles like T-shirts, basecaps etc. which articulate some issue of short-lived popular interest. You simply haven't got the normal amount of time it takes to register a new company.
- This kind of registration is less expensive, too.

Disadvantages
- A possible disadvantage is that some claims exist against the company you bought. It could be a complicated matter to get out of liability for such claims.
- Because the company is no longer trading, it is more difficult to carry out due diligence.

UNIT 2

page 17

1 1 Confidentiality
2 Competition
3 Duration of contract/ Term of employment
4 Absence
5 Leave entitlement
6 Duties
7 Applicable law
8 Severance

page 18

2 1 i
2 g
3 e
4 a
5 j
6 b
7 c
8 d
9 f
10 h

3 1 false
2 true
3 true
4 false
5 true
6 true
7 false
8 false

page 19

4 1 No. Clause 1 says that other places of work are always of a temporary nature. The manager must decide how long the project group will meet in Lucerne or how long one particular employee should have to work there. She can't send the same employee there week after week.
2 No. According to clause 3(2) compensation for

overtime solely by payment is possible even if it is not typical. The management can refuse but it can't do this unreasonably. If a manager simply says that he doesn't have time to discuss the matter, this is not reasonable.

3 Probably not. If the boyfriend and the employee live together all the time (i.e. he doesn't have his own separate home), then he is her partner. Clause 4.1 states that the employee is entitled to take her leave in the school holidays if her partner is tied to these holidays because of his/her profession. This is because he is a school teacher.

4 Yes. According to clause 5 the sick note must be handed in no later than four calendar days after the start of the period of absence. Saturday and Sunday are calendar days, so the sick note arrived late.

5 Probably the employer. The note written by the Spanish doctor to the employee's doctor back in England is not a formal sick note in the sense of clause 5. It simply contains some information about the medication which the patient was given. However, there might be scope here for the employer and the employee to find a compromise.

6 He is right. Clause 6 states that the employee has a right to paid time off if the vaccination is made necessary by a business trip. In this case, the vaccination is made necessary by a holiday so the employee must have the vaccination in his or her own time.

5
1 I apologise
2 contacting
3 Unfortunately
4 returned
5 I am attaching
6 resolve
7 reasonably
8 wish
9 discuss
10 please

page 20

6 (suggested answer)
Working hours: Cathy has basically got what she wanted. Although the contract still doesn't say specifically that the normal week is Monday to Friday, it says this indirectly because weekend work is referred to as being necessary "from time to time".

Leave entitlement: This is definitely not what she wanted. According to this, she can only carry seven days' leave over into the following year and only up to the beginning of March.

Remuneration: This is exactly what she wanted.

page 21

7
a Perhaps I could suggest a compromise here?
b I am happy with the suggested amendments to clauses 1.2 and 4.5.
c Please let me know if this might be possible.
d It would also give me an extra month in which to take it.
e As it stands, I would still risk losing up to eight days' leave a year.
f Thank you for sending me the contract amendments yesterday.
g Furthermore, I would have to take any unused leave by the end of February.
h Would you agree to ten days, to be taken by the end of March?
i This would guarantee me a minimum of 25 days' leave.
j However, I am a little concerned about the leave entitlement clause.

The correct order is:
1 f 2 b 3 j 4 e 5 g 6 a 7 h
8 i 9 d 10 c

page 22

8 (suggested answer)
Cathy has given notice in writing and her written notice is addressed to the correct person. However, she has misunderstood the period of notice in her contract. She can only start a new job on the 1st of March.

page 23

9
1 e (right)
2 f (right)
3 d (obligation)
4 a (right)
5 b (right)
6 c (obligation)

page 24

10 Statement 3 best sums up what is said.

The following statements are true:
1 a 2 b 3 b, c 4 b, c

UNIT 3

page 26

Preamble

"What happens if, after the parties have signed, we find that there's a mistake in a contract – say about VAT? Do we have to draw up a whole new contract?"

There should be a *severance* clause in a contract. This clause makes it clear that if one particular clause in the contract turns out to be an error or invalid for some other reason, the rest of the contract remains unaffected. The severance clause usually goes on to state that the two parties will replace the invalid clause with a clause that is valid and comes as close as possible to the original intention of the parties.

"Let's say there's a rail strike and we fail to deliver our goods to the client. I assume we're protected by the *force majeure* clause, aren't we?"

Not necessarily. If a rail strike went on for two weeks and you made no effort to transport the goods to the client in some other way – even though other forms of transport might have been possible – the *force majeure* clause won't protect you.

"We had a big order from a client and the client said it was OK to ask a third party to supply part of the order for us. But are we liable if the third party's goods are defective?"

It's possible. It all depends on how the *assignment* clause is worded. If liability is not explicitly transferred to the third party in the wording, then it rests with the original party to the contract. So Party A (the client) might make a claim against Party B (the other party to the contract) in respect of defective goods delivered by Party C (the third party). Party B would then, in turn, have to make a claim against Party C!

"I often see "terms and conditions" in our sales documentation. Aren't they just two words for the same thing?"

Yes and no. In a non-specialist context "terms and conditions" is one of these noun pairs like "life and limb" or "peace and quiet" – to be understood as a single unit of meaning. However, for a lawyer "terms" can be "conditions" or "warranties". If Party A breaches a condition, then Party B has no continuing obligations under the contract. However, if Party A breaches a warranty, then Party B can claim damages for this breach but the contract remains in force.

"A client agreed to buy some goods from us but he needed them urgently. He didn't have time to wait for all the paperwork to be drawn up and signed. I sent him the goods and he paid – no problem. But was he actually legally bound by our verbal agreement?"

In this situation the verbal agreement was binding. Problems arise, of course, if the two parties recall the details of their verbal agreement differently.

"I keep coming across this word "consideration" in contracts. Does it mean that you have – sort of – thought carefully about the other party's offer before signing the contract?"

No, it doesn't. Consideration is Party B's performance in return for Party A's goods or services. Consideration is usually in the form of money but doesn't have to be. Party A might sell his motorbike to Party B. As consideration, Party B might agree to repair the roof of Party A's house.

1 1 High-performance LCD screens.
2 Pixeltechnik GmbH
3 Annex 1
4 Digital View plc.

page 28

2 1 thereafter
2 thereof
3 hereinafter
4 hereto
5 therein
6 thereunder
7 hereby
8 therewith

page 29

3 a 8 b 4 c 3 d 6 e 1
f 5 g 2 h 7

page 30

4 1 administrator
2 comply with
3 terms
4 invoke
5 winding-up petition
6 warranty
7 indemnify
8 exceed
9 binding
10 set out

page 31

5 1 Just a question about the penalty clause. Can we reduce the price by 1% if Pixeltechnik delivers four days' late?

Actually, you can reduce the price by the full 2%. The contract states: " ... for every week or **part thereof**". This means that any part of a week – even if it is one day – entitles the purchaser to invoke the penalty clause and charge the full 2%.

2 Where exactly does it say in this contract how many items we have to order?

It is all set out in Annex 2. (see 3.1)

3 Where can we find all the prices for the different LCD screens?

This is all set out in Annex 2. (see 4.1)

4 I'm just looking at clause 4. Can Pixeltechnik increase the price if it wants to?

No. The prices are fixed for the full period of the agreement. (see 4.1)

5 I'm a little unclear about clause 5. Is this a two-year contract or not?

It is a two-year contract but it will be renewed for one additional year unless either of the parties terminates the contract (see 5.2).

6 What exactly are our rights if Pixeltechnik goes bankrupt?

You can terminate the contract with 21 days' notice. (see 8.1(iii))

7 There's something in clause 10 I'd like to clarify. What happens if some goods are defective? Can we insist on a replacement?

Yes, you can. (see 10.2)

8 What happens if another company suddenly claims that it owns the patent on Pixeltechnik's LCD screen technology? Can we be sued by this company?

No you can't. Clause 11.1 protects you against this risk.

6 1 found
2 reached
3 listed
4 arising
5 imposed
6 leading
7 failing
8 claimed

page 32

7 • What is the problem?

Pixeltechnik has to recall 10 batches of 500 items each because they are defective.

• How quickly can Pixeltechnik solve the problem?

They guarantee to deliver all 5,000 items within 21 days.

• Is the tone appropriate?

Definitely. Polite and apologetic.

• Is the information sufficient?

In some ways not. It is not clear how many items will be delivered between the 10th and the 21st day. The letter is also a bit vague about the cause of the problem. The client would want to be reassured that there isn't a serious technical problem that might turn out to be difficult to solve.

page 33

8 The advice would probably be to invoke the penalty clause. If Digital View is going to experience serious production difficulties because of this delay, it might feel entitled to some further compensation. Furthermore, Digital View might have to offer some kind of discount to its customers to compensate them for late delivery. In such a situation, Digital View would be justified in seeking to recover these additional costs from Pixeltechnik, too. This is something that would have to be negotiated.

9 Part 1
1 true
2 false (The production manager noticed that the sampling results were a problem.)
3 false (He is not completely sure. He uses the word "probably".)
4 false (They carried out tests every day but didn't notice the problem for ten days.)
5 true

9 Part 2
1 – He agreed a new delivery schedule.
– He delivered the 5,000 screens on time and the quality was fine.
– He paid 15,000 euros penalty to Digital View.
2 Digital View is seeking to terminate the contract with 21 days' notice.
3 It is invoking 8.1(i), which makes reference to unsatisfactory performance as a reason for terminating the contract.
4 Pixeltechnik is only going to cover its costs after two years. If the contract is terminated now, before the two years are over, Pixeltechnik will make a loss. A third year would be necessary for Pixeltechnik to make any profit.

page 34

10 (suggested answer)
1 a Since Herr Hörner used the word "defective" in his letter to Digital View, the purchaser would naturally have assumed that the goods were defective in terms of the contractual specifications. In any case, Herr Hörner is a little unclear about how "defective" the 5,000 screens were.
1 b The fact that a compromise seemed to have been reached favours Pixeltechnik. Digital View's good faith seems to be in question here.
2 It depends how difficult the consequences of the product recall were for Digital View. If the problems they encountered with their clients were such as to put these client relationships at risk, then Digital View has a point. If Digital View managed to resolve any problems with clients amicably, then, given the penalty paid by Pixeltechnik anyway, its attempts to terminate the contract early could be seen as unreasonable.
3 The concept of "reasonableness" is important. In principle, contracting parties should behave reasonably to one another.
4 Digital View doesn't have to go into a third year if it doesn't want to. It must, however, observe its obligations for the full term of two years - unless it can reasonably claim "unsatisfactory performance". In order to terminate the contract after two years, it must give written notice of its intention to terminate no later than 90 days before the end of the two-year period.
5 A dispute resolution clause would certainly have been helpful to Pixeltechnik. The contract has an "Applicable law and jurisdiction" clause. This means that disputes have to be settled in the court of law stated in the clause. As this is an English court, a legal dispute would involve some degree of inconvenience and extra cost for Pixeltechnik.

Ultimately, the solicitors' advice will depend on the size of the loss Pixeltechnik will have to bear if Digital View is allowed to terminate the contract now. A court case would be time-consuming and potentially costly. However, if Pixeltechnik's loss is going to be considerable i.e. in the hundreds of thousands of euros, legal action would certainly seem sensible. In any case, Pixeltechnik is well advised to make sure any future contracts contain a dispute resolution clause.

11
1 *in*valid
2 *un*lawful
3 *un*enforceable
4 *dis*satisfied
5 *ir*reconcilable
6 *un*affected
7 *in*effective
8 *un*foreseeable
9 *im*partial
10 *un*confirmed
11 *in*correct
12 *in*complete
13 *un*reasonable
14 *un*satisfactory

page 35

13 Task 1 – The case about the house is clear cut. Mr. Blue rejected the original offer and made a counter-offer. The vendor of the house rejected Mr. Blue's counter-offer. In no way is he bound by his original offer because this offer was rejected.

Task 2 – The swimming pool case is more complex. Clearly the swimming pool is safe to use even though it isn't quite as deep as the owner wanted it to be. Some courts would suggest that the owner accept compensation. Others might side with the owner and insist that the whole swimming pool be rebuilt at the expense of the construction company. What happened in this particular case was that the owner was required to accept compensation. Once again, the concept of "reasonableness" was an important factor in this decision.

14
1 defective
2 terminate
3 binding
4 specifications
5 terms
6 comply
7 invoke
8 expire

UNIT 4

page 37

Preamble

- A new drug substance. Patent (limited to 20 years from date of registration, the so-called priority date, not date of market launch)
- A 19th century violin concerto. The published music score would be covered by copyright but the music itself was composed too long ago. The descendants of the composer would have no rights to royalties.
- A new perfume. The bottle, and the name would be protected by design rights and trade marks. However, it is difficult to protect a smell.
- A scientific theory e.g. $e = mc^2$. The theory itself cannot be protected, only any commercial applications.
- A distinctive chocolate product. Such a product would have trade mark protection and possibly design right protection, too.
- A TV news show format. Difficult. One could argue that a news show is of such a universal nature that you can't protect it. However, if it has certain very

identifiable special features, these might be able to be protected by copyright.

- A new novel. Copyright.
- A sauce or a drink with an unmistakeable flavour e.g. HP sauce or Coca-Cola. Trade mark protection. Beyond this, Coca-Cola protects the recipe of its drink by simply keeping it a secret. The handful of executives who know the formula are never allowed to fly together!
- A new type of toaster. A patent. In the case of this particular toaster, the student who invented it entered it for a design competition. Unfortunately, this placed his invention in the public domain. The student had not yet patented his invention, so it was no longer patentable.
- A photo of St. Stephen's cathedral in Vienna at sundown. Difficult. The photograph itself is protected by copyright. If someone copies it out of a book and uses it without the photographer's permission, this is a copyright infringement. However, the image of the cathedral is universally accessible and so can't be protected unless the composition of the photograph is particularly original. This is a very important source of protection to photographers who take highly innovative pictures. It would be unfair for someone to just stand in the same position, recreate the image and then offer it on the market at a knock-down price.

page 38

1 1 format 2 damages 3 general 4 copyright 5 patented 6 competitor 7 infringement 8 validity 9 plaintiff 10 trade mark

2 a This is a case about **copyright** and went all the way to appeal. The plaintiff claimed that his copyright existed in the scripts to his show and in the format. His problem was that he was required by law to demonstrate that his show should enjoy protection as "an original dramatic work". The court took the view that a talent show is something that can't enjoy copyright protection because this would be unjust to anyone else who wanted to do a talent show on TV. In its view, Mr. Green's show, despite the catchphrases and some distinctive format features, remained a talent show and, therefore, undeserving of copyright protection.

b This is a case about **patents**. The Court of Appeal found that the patent was indeed valid. Something that may seem obvious with hindsight might not have been obvious at all before it was done. Generally, this question of obviousness seems to be a problem in patent law that refuses to go away.

c This is a case about **trade mark** protection. The court decided that, despite the name change made by the defendant, the "likelihood of confusion" still existed. It found for the plaintiff.

page 40

3 1 false 2 true 3 true 4 false 5 false

4 1 sole 2 desires 3 acquired 4 granted 5 set forth 6 warrants 7 commence 8 expires 9 permissible 10 consent

page 40/41

5 1 1 May 2 3.1 3 8 4 5 5 5.2 6 3

page 42

6

Express a contrast	*However / Nevertheless*
Provide additional information	*Moreover*
Express a consequence	*As a result*
State an opinion	*In my view*
Restate or reformulate some information	*In other words*

7 1 Moreover 2 However 3 As a result 4 In other words 5 Nevertheless / However

8 1 true 2 false 3 true 4 false 5 true

page 43

9 1 purchaser 2 rights holder 3 publisher 4 80,000 5 40,000 6 three months 7 one year 8 40,000

page 44

10 1 The payment period you suggest is a little too short / isn't quite long enough.
2 I think our share of the royalties is a little too low / isn't really high enough.
3 I don't think that's very practical.
4 If you extended the licence area to include Japan, we would / could / might accept royalties of 4%.
5 I don't think our board would agree to that.

page 44/45

11 1 a, b 2 c 3 b 4 b 5 a

page 46

13 1 ownership 2 publisher 3 unauthorised 4 adaptations 5 holder 6 financial 7 infringement 8 loser 9 inspiration 10 creator 11 permission 12 criticism

The court found for J. K. Rowling and Warner Bros., stating that the publication of the encyclopaedia wourld cause Rowling "irreparable harm".

UNIT 5

page 48

Preamble

1 In favour of more regulation. An employee, possibly a member of the union or the works council.
2 Not in favour of more regulation. Possibly a director of a company or a business analyst.

3 Slightly unclear. Sounds as if he sees the OFT as something that, in reality, doesn't make much difference. Probably the director of a company.
4 The owner / director of a company that was taken over. Not in favour of more regulation. Very happy with the way things turned out for his company.

page 49

1 1 merger
2 results
3 acquired
4 takeover
5 targeted
6 expansion

2 1 false (He finds the company's documentation on M&A procedures confusing.)
2 false (There is documentation on both.)
3 true

page 50

3 2 f 3 h 4 a 5 c 6 d 7 g
8 b 9 e

page 51

4 Changes to information:
Step f: Regina needs to add that for small acquisitions (up to 2 million euros) the supervisory board does not need to be consulted.

Step c: The CEO can represent the company but only with another board member or an authorised signatory.

Step e: For those acquisitions for which the supervisory board needs to be consulted, the necessary majority of represented equity capital is now 75%.

page 52

5 1 NDAs set out the obligations of those persons who come into contact with certain information. The agreement sets out in detail all the things that these persons are not allowed to do with this information. The agreement also specifies a fine if its terms are breached. The fine does not exclude the injured party's rights to seek further damages in a civil action. Generally quite effective but the burden of proof lies with the injured party.
2 LOIs do create obligations and very often include a fine that must be paid if either party is in breach of the terms of the LOI. Civil actions for damages beyond the fine paid are not excluded unless this is specifically stated. LOIs are good at giving parties some assurance that a complicated process (e.g. a planned merger) that will cost time and money is being taken seriously by the other party. However, they provide no guarantee that a particular contract will actually come into being.
3 The SEC would become suspicious if there were unusual patterns of trading in a particular company's shares. They would have the right to check if any of the names on the insider list had been involved in share transactions after the date on which, for example, they became aware of confidential information that could affect the price of a company's shares. Proving that a criminal offence has been committed can, however, be extremely difficult.
4 Not everything is entrusted to the free market. Think of the Law Society or the General Medical Council. These bodies have the exclusive right to regulate their respective professions. A competitor organisation isn't allowed to offer the same services.

6
UK
The *GmbH & Co. KG* is broadly similar to a limited liability partnership in the UK. But it is also unlike the UK limited liability partnership because one of its partners – the partner with unlimited liability – is a limited liability company.

The mini-GmbH is similar to the English limited because you only need EUR 1 of equity capital to form the company. It is also different because it is seen as a transition to a full GmbH. The company must put 25% of its annual profits into its equity capital until it has the EUR 25,000 to become a full GmbH.

The German *Rechtsanwalt* is comparable to the English solicitor but the two are not quite the same. In England there are a lot of courts where the solicitor is not allowed to argue his client's case. This work must be done by a barrister.

US
The fee system for German lawyers in civil claims is unlike the system for US attorneys. In Germany the fee does not depend on the size of the damages awarded by the court.

The *Vorstand* and *Aufsichtsrat* are comparable to the board of management in the US but they are also different. In the US the non-executive directors sit with the executive directors on a single board of management.

page 53

7
- "Resolution" does not collocate with allocate and enter.
  The two synonyms are *pass* and *carry*.
- "Approval" does not collocate with *select* and *acquire*.
  The two synonyms are *withhold* and *refuse*.
- "Agreement" does not collocate with *assume* and *inform*.
  The two synonyms are *break* and *violate*.
- "Meeting" does not collocate with *resolve* and *make*.
  The two synonyms are *call* and *convene*.

8 1 reject / resolution
2 seek / approval
3 convene / meeting
4 draw up / agreement
5 attend / meeting
6 withhold / approval

page 54

9 Part 1
a Name of company: No Frills
Paid-up capital: £300,000
Founded in: 2005
Current debts: nil
Type of company: limited
Current no. of cafés: 16
No. of shareholders: 3
Style of cafés: retro
Country of registration: England
b They are short. When they expire the landlord may want to demand a much higher rent.

c Regina will ask the solicitors in England to check again the lease agreements and the market commercial rents in the relevant locations. Regina and Oliver will then quantify the risk.

9 Part 2

a He would like to pay them in the form of *Esskultur* shares.
b It would still be a limited company. It would now be a wholly owned subsidiary of *Esskultur AG*.
c The existing shareholders must agree with a majority of 75% to waive their right to a new share issue.
d They think that the bank's interest rates might be unattractive. The repayments would also burden the company for a number of years.
e It does if it wants to take out more than EUR 2 million.
f Because it may need major investment soon and this money should come from the capital reserve.

page 55

10 1 d 2 b 3 a 4 h 5 e 6 c
7 f 8 g

page 56

11 1 true
2 true (This is made clear in 4 (2).)
3 true
4 true
5 false (The seller also has the right to make claims in addition to the stated amount of 50,000 euros.)

UNIT 6

page 58

Preamble

Trade marks need to be monitored in case of passing off. **Patents** need to be monitored because they expire. A product's profitability is inevitably affected when it is no longer protected by a patent. Legal challenges to patents can also represent a risk. A company may have to invest a lot of money to defend its patent rights in court.

Warranties can represent a risk, especially towards the end of the warranty period. Realistic sums for repair, maintenance and replacement of defective goods need to be set aside to cover this risk.

A **company pension scheme** can quickly represent a risk to a company if it has, on the one hand, a contractual commitment to provide a particular pension scheme but, on the other hand, has not done enough to ensure that the necessary funds are really available. This happens to more companies than one might think.

Contracts with suppliers can represent a risk in all kinds of ways. The quality of the supplier's goods and services may be a problem or the completion of work by specific deadlines. The relevant contracts have to be drafted very carefully to ensure that, if the supplier's performance is unsatisfactory, the damage and inconvenience caused to the other party can be kept to a minimum.

Equipment represents a risk because it wears out or becomes obsolete. Moreover, the tax advantage from its depreciation is only available for a limited number of years.

Compliance with the **corporate code** can be extremely important. We only need to think of companies like Enron, where executive standards were not as high as they should have been, to see the enormous damage that can be done to a company and its reputation. Closer to home, a certain supermarket discounter could have avoided damaging publicity if they had monitored adherence to data protection legislation more carefully and a well-known DAX company could have prevented a long and painful period of introspection if it had monitored compliance with its own guidelines on the payment of bribes.

Employment legislation is always a risk factor. A company needs to understand exactly what its obligations are, so that it can manage its staff without fear of being overruled by a court of law.

Health and safety legislation represents a risk because new processes or facilities may be more expensive to design because of this legislation or may be constructed and then not allowed to go into use because of compliance problems.

1 1 b 2 e 3 f 4 a 5 d 6 c

page 59

2 1 bail out
2 drawn on
3 set back
4 go under
5 put up
6 write off
7 wind up
8 wipe out

page 60

4 1 She thinks they are too focused on health and safety and insurance issues and not enough on commercial, financial and legal issues.

2 i) Over-reliance on major clients is a risk if the major client becomes insolvent or simply decides to use a new supplier. ii) Exchange rate fluctuations can wipe out the profit on a transaction. iii) It is a risk to have a sum of money secured against an asset where the asset, if realized, cannot cover the sum secured on it. This could force the company into insolvency if it got into financial difficulties and was unable to service its debts.

3 Florian Wenger would look at risk management from a legal point of view.

page 61

5 1 a* 2 c 3 b

* "I see where you're coming from" is sometimes a polite way of signalling disagreement.

6 For answers see exercise 7 below.

page 62

7 Clauses 2 and 5
These clauses are from a leasehold agreement. The automatic renewal clause is a risk because there is then no chance to renegotiate the agreement. The lawyer recommends terminating the agreement whilst at the same time signalling that one wishes to negotiate a new leasehold agreement. Another important reason for renegotiating is the fact that the company is holding an option on – and paying for – 200 m^2 of office space which it probably doesn't need.

The link between the rent and the Consumer Price Index is only fair if commercial rents are rising in line with inflation. This is not the case in this particular district of Vienna. Basically, the company is paying 10% to 15% more rent than the market rate.

Clause 3
This clause comes from a works council agreement, which supplements the contract of employment. This is a fairly generous compensation package and would be very expensive for the company if it had to make staff redundant. The company should renegotiate with the works council.

Clause 6
This clause comes from a company acquisition agreement. Basically, it makes clear that *Form and Function* might have to pay an additional sum for a company it recently acquired. The company should find out how large this sum might be and should make provision for this.

page 63

8
1. At no time **was my client** made aware of the true financial circumstances of your client's company when he signed the contract.
2. Seldom **does one come** across an employment contract with as many loopholes as this.
3. **It is** the whole question of misrepresentation **that** interests me in this case.
4. **What** the members of this union find particularly unfair **is** that the company is considering cuts after such a successful year.
5. **What** I find suspicious in this case **is** that the company was registered in the Cayman Islands.
6. The rest of the clause is fine. However, **it is** the last sentence **that** is open to interpretation.

9
1. Collapse in orders / insolvency of two major clients
2. They refused to support a debt restructuring plan.
3. Form and Function GmbH is thought to be a major supplier and could be affected by this bankruptcy.

page 64

10
1. false (An administration order means that an attempt will be made to rescue the company. A winding-up order means that the company will be liquidated.)
2. true
3. false (The repayment problems first began six months ago.)
4. true
5. true
6. false (She thinks the lawyer is right but she isn't sure that getting the furniture back will benefit the company.)
7. true
8. true (By implication. She says that the company should be able to keep its core business intact.)

11 The mortgage on Ranjit's flat and the loan secured on it do not exceed the value of the flat. If Ranjit can find an alternative source of income quickly, he should be able to continue to meet his mortgage and loan obligations. If he does this, the secured creditors will have no need to force him to sell his home.

Ranjit has made progress in paying off both the loan and the mortgage, so will be seen as creditworthy.

If he realizes his receivables and his inventory, he will have EUR 18,000.

As employees are preferential creditors, they will be entitled to EUR 6,000.

The remaining sum of EUR 12,000 would be available to be distributed amongst the unsecured creditors.

There is nothing to be gained by the unsecured creditors seeking to force Ranjit to sell his home – even if this were possible – because its value would only be sufficient to satisfy the claims of the secured creditors.

Assuming that Ranjit finds an alternative source of income, he would be required to make further payments to the unsecured creditors for a number of years.

page 65

12
1. secured
2. asset
3. distribute
4. preferential
5. unsecured
6. repayment

13
1. insolvent
2. lease
3. severance
4. acquisition
5. debts
6. loss

page 66

14
1. If the new machine in the company's warehouse **hadn't been** paid for, it **wouldn't have been** part of the insolvency estate.
2. If the bank **hadn't secured** its loan against assets of the company, it **wouldn't have got** most of its money back.
3. If the creditors **had had** confidence in the company's ability to pay, they **wouldn't have petitioned** the court to make a winding-up order.
4. If the directors **had delayed** in registering the company insolvent, they **would have been** guilty of a criminal offence.
5. If the company **hadn't got** into a lot of speculative non-core ventures, its core business **wouldn't have been** exposed to risk.
6. If it **hadn't been** a company with limited liability, the members' personal assets **would have been** at risk.

pages 68–69

Test yourself!

Across
3 renumeration
5 equity
7 comply
8 invoke
10 sue
12 partnership
17 articles
18 binding
19 waive
20 freelancer
21 patentee
23 infringement
25 force majeure
28 amendment
29 realize

Down
1 prior
2 resolution
4 insolvent
6 issue
9 preferential
11 instalment
13 royalties
14 specifications
15 void
16 entitled
20 form
22 security
24 target
26 consent
27 assets

A–Z wordlist

A	to **abandon** [ə'bændən]	verlassen, im Stich lassen
	abridged [ə'brɪdʒd]	gekürzt
	absence ['æbsəns]	Abwesenheit
	accidental damage [æksɪˌdentl 'dæmɪdʒ]	Unfallschaden, unabsichtlich verursachter Schaden
	accordance, in ~ with [ə'kɔ:dəns]	gemäß, in Übereinstimmung mit
	accountancy [ə'kaʊntənsi]	Rechnungswesen, Buchhaltung
	accounting [ə'kaʊntɪŋ]	Buchführung, Buchhaltung
	to **accrue** [ə'kru:]	(Überstunden:) anfallen, auflaufen
	to **acquire** [ə'kwaɪə]	erwerben, kaufen
	acquisition [ˌækwɪ'zɪʃn]	Erwerb, Übernahme
	actionable ['ækʃnəbl]	verklagbar, belangbar
	adjustment [ə'dʒʌstmənt]	Anpassung
	to **administer** [əd'mɪnɪstə]	verwalten
	administration [ədˌmɪnɪ'streɪʃn]	Konkursverwaltung
	administration charge [ədˌmɪnɪ'streɪʃn tʃɑ:dʒ]	Verwaltungsgebühr
	administration order [ədˌmɪnɪ'streɪʃn ɔ:də]	Konkurseröffnungsbeschluss
	administration, to **go into ~** [ədmɪnɪ'streɪʃn]	in Konkurs gehen
	administrator [əd'mɪnɪstreɪtə]	Konkursverwalter/in
	advisable [əd'vaɪzəbl]	ratsam
	advocacy ['ædvəkəsi]	Anwaltstätigkeit
	to **affect** [ə'fekt]	beeinflussen, beeinträchtigen
	affected, to **be ~ by sth** [ə'fektɪd]	von etw betroffen sein
	aforementioned [əˌfɔ:'menʃənd]	obengenannt
	agreement [ə'gri:mənt]	Vereinbarung, Einigung
	allegation [ˌælə'geɪʃn]	Anschuldigung, Vorwurf
	alleged [ə'ledʒd]	angeblich, mutmaßlich
	to **allocate** ['æləkeɪt]	zuteilen
	alteration [ˌɔ:ltə'reɪʃn]	Änderung
	amendment [ə'mendmənt]	Änderung, Zusatz
	annex ['æneks]	Anhang
	to **announce** [ə'naʊns]	ankündigen
	annual general meeting (AGM) [ˌænjuəl ˌdʒenrəl 'mi:tɪŋ]	Jahreshauptversammlung
	annual leave [ˌænjuəl 'li:v]	Jahresurlaub
	annual statement [ˌænjuəl 'steɪtmənt]	Jahresabschluss
	to **anticipate** [æn'tɪsɪpeɪt]	vorhersehen, rechnen mit
	appeal, to **go to ~** [ə'pi:l]	in Berufung/Revision gehen, Rechtsmittel einlegen
	applicability [əˌplɪkə'bɪləti]	Anwendbarkeit
	applicable law [əˌplɪkəbl 'lɔ:]	geltendes Recht
	application [ˌæplɪ'keɪʃn]	Antrag
	to **apply** [ə'plaɪ]	(Gesetz etc.:) gelten
	to **apply for sth** [ə'plaɪ fə]	etw beantragen
	to **appoint sb** [ə'pɔɪnt]	jdn ernennen, einstellen
	appointment [ə'pɔɪntmənt]	Termin; Ernennung, Berufung
	to **appreciate sth** [ə'pri:ʃieɪt]	sich einer Sache bewusst sein
	arbitrator ['ɑ:bɪtreɪtə]	Vermittler/in, Schlichter/in
	articles of association [ˌɑ:tɪklz əv əˌsəʊsi'eɪʃn]	Gesellschaftsvertrag, Satzung
	to **ascertain** [ˌæsə'teɪn]	feststellen, bestimmen
	to **assess sth** [ə'ses]	etw einschätzen, abschätzen
	assessment [ə'sesmənt]	Bewertung, Abschätzung
	assets ['æsets]	Vermögen, Vermögenswerte
	to **assign sth to sb** [ə'saɪn]	(Rechte) jdm etw übertragen
	assignee [əˌsaɪ'ni:]	Beauftragte/r
	assumed, to **be ~ to be sth** [ə'sju:md]	für etw gehalten werden
	attorney (AE) [ə'tɜ:ni]	Anwalt/Anwältin
	audit ['ɔ:dɪt]	(Über-)Prüfung, Revision
	to **authorize** ['ɔ:θəraɪz]	bevollmächtigen
	authorized signatory [ˌɔ:θəraɪzd 'sɪgnətri]	Unterschriftsberechtigte/r
	authority [ɔ:'θɒrəti]	Vollmacht
B	**backlog of work** [ˌbæklɒg əv 'wɜ:k]	unerledigte Arbeit
	to **bail sb out** [ˌbeɪl 'aʊt]	jdn sanieren, retten
	balance ['bæləns]	Rest(betrag)
	ban [bæn]	Verbot
	to **ban sb from doing sth** [bæn]	jdm untersagen/verbieten, etw zu tun
	to **bankrupt sb** ['bæŋkrʌpt]	jdn in den Konkurs treiben, ruinieren
	bankrupt, to **become ~** ['bæŋkrʌpt]	in Konkurs gehen
	bankruptcy ['bæŋkrʌpsi]	Konkurs, Pleite
	bankruptcy petition ['bæŋkrʌpsi pətɪʃn]	Konkursantrag
	batch [bætʃ]	Los, Serie
	to **bear liability** [ˌbeə laɪə'bɪləti]	haften, haftbar sein
	behalf, on ~ of sb [ɒn bɪ'hɑ:f əv]	in jds Namen
	behaviour [bɪ'heɪvjə]	Verhalten
	bid [bɪd]	Angebot, Offerte
	bidder ['bɪdə]	Bieter, Kaufinteressent
	binding ['baɪndɪŋ]	verbindlich, bindend
	binding effect [ˌbaɪndɪŋ ɪ'fekt]	bindende Wirkung
	board (of management) [ˌbɔ:d əv 'mænɪdʒmənt]	Vorstand, Unternehmensleitung
	body ['bɒdi]	Behörde, Organisation
	branch office ['brɑ:ntʃ ɒfɪs]	Niederlassung
	to **breach** [bri:tʃ]	verstoßen gegen
	breach of contract [ˌbri:tʃ əv 'kɒntrækt]	Vertragsbruch, Vertragsverletzung
	brief [bri:f]	Schriftsatz
	to **bring an action against sb** [ˌbrɪŋ ən 'ækʃn]	jdn verklagen
	broadcast fee ['brɔ:dkɑ:st fi:]	Lizenzgebühr, GEMA-Gebühr
	buildings and contents insurance [ˌbɪldɪŋ ən 'kɒntənts ɪnʃʊərəns]	Gebäude- und Inhaltsversicherung
	business organization [ˌbɪznəs ˌɔ:gənaɪ'zeɪʃn]	Unternehmen
	to **butt in** [ˌbʌt 'ɪn]	unterbrechen, einhaken
	to **buy sb out** [ˌbaɪ 'aʊt]	jdn auszahlen
C	**candlepower** ['kændlpaʊə]	Lichtstärke
	capital reserves ['kæpɪtl rɪˌzɜ:vz]	Kapitalreserven
	case [keɪs]	Fall, Prozesssache
	case law ['keɪs lɔ:]	Präzedenzrecht, Fallrecht
	to **cease** [si:s]	aufhören, einstellen, beenden
	to **cease trading** [ˌsi:s 'treɪdɪŋ]	den Geschäftsbetrieb einstellen
	CEO (Chief Executive Officer) [ˌtʃi:f ɪg'zekjətɪv 'ɒfɪsə]	Vorstandsvorsitzender, Hauptgeschäftsführer
	certificated [sə'tɪfɪkeɪtɪd]	bescheinigt, beglaubigt
	to **certify** ['sɜ:tɪfaɪ]	beglaubigen
	chain [tʃeɪn]	Kette
	charge [tʃɑ:dʒ]	(gesicherte) Forderung, Belastung
	to **charge (a price)** [tʃɑ:dʒ]	(einen Preis) berechnen, verlangen
	to **charge sb with sb** [tʃɑ:dʒ]	jdn wegen einer Sache anklagen, jdn einer Sache beschuldigen
	chargeholder ['tʃɑ:dʒhəʊldə]	gesicherte/r Gläubiger/in
	civil law partnership [ˌsɪvl 'lɔ: pɑ:tnəʃɪp]	Gesellschaft bürgerlichen Rechts (GbR)
	claim [kleɪm]	Forderung, Anspruch, Schadenersatzanspruch
	to **claim** [kleɪm]	erklären, behaupten
	to **claim damages** [ˌkleɪm 'dæmɪdʒɪz]	Schadenersatzansprüche stellen

claimant ['kleɪmənt]	Beschwerdeführer/in, Kläger/in
clause [klɔ:z]	Klausel
clearance certificate ['klɪərəns sətɪfɪkət]	Genehmigung
counsel ['kaʊnsl]	Anwalt/Anwältin
to **co-opt** [ˌkəʊ'ɒpt]	zweckentfremden
codified law [ˌkəʊdɪfaɪd 'lɔ:]	kodifiziertes Recht
to **combat sth** ['kɒmbæt]	etw bekämpfen
to **commence** [kə'mens]	beginnen, anfangen
to **commence trading** [kəˌmens 'treɪdɪŋ]	den Geschäftsbetrieb aufnehmen
commencement [kə'mensmənt]	Beginn, Anfang
commercial objectives [kəˌmɜ:ʃl əb'dʒektɪvz]	wirtschaftliche Ziele
commercial property [kəˌmɜ:ʃl 'prɒpəti]	Geschäftsimmobilien
commercial register [kəˌmɜ:ʃl 'redʒɪstə]	Handelsregister
to **commission** [kə'mɪʃn]	in Auftrag geben
commitment [kə'mɪtmənt]	Verpflichtung, Zusage
commodity [kə'mɒdəti]	Ware
company law ['kʌmpəni lɔ:]	Gesellschaftsrecht, Aktienrecht
company policy [ˌkʌmpəni 'pɒləsi]	Unternehmenspolitik
to **compensate sb for sth** ['kɒmpenseɪt]	jdn für etw entschädigen
compensation [ˌkɒmpən'seɪʃn]	Ausgleich, Entschädigung; Entgelt, Vergütung
compère ['kɒmpeə]	Ansager/in
competition [ˌkɒmpə'tɪʃn]	Konkurrenz, Konkurrenten, Wettbewerb
competitor [kəm'petɪtə]	Konkurrent, Wettbewerber
completion (of a deal) [kəm'pli:ʃn]	Abschluss (eines Geschäfts)
compliance [kəm'plaɪəns]	Vertragstreue; Einhaltung, Befolgung (eines Gesetzes)
compliance code [kəm'plaɪəns kəʊd]	Verhaltenskodex
to **comply with sth** [kəm'plaɪ]	etw befolgen, einer Sache nachkommen
compulsory liquidation [kəmˌpʌlsəri lɪkwɪ'deɪʃn]	Zwangsauflösung
to **conclude (a contract)** [kən'klu:d]	(einen Vertrag) abschließen
condition [kən'dɪʃn]	wesentliche Vertragsbestimmung
conditional upon [kənˌdɪʃənl ə'pɒn]	abhänging von
confidentiality [ˌkɒnfɪˌdenʃi'æləti]	Vertraulichkeit
confrontational [ˌkɒnfrʌn'teɪʃənl]	konfrontativ
consent [kən'sent]	Einwilligung, Zustimmung
to **consent** [kən'sent]	zustimmen, einwilligen
considerable [kən'sɪdərəbl]	erheblich
consideration [kənˌsɪdə'reɪʃn]	Gegenleistung; Entgelt, Vergütung
consideration, under ~ [ʌndə kənˌsɪdə'reɪʃn]	vorliegend, in Betracht kommend
consistent, to **be ~ with sth** [kən'sɪstənt]	mit etw vereinbar sein, mit etw übereinstimmen
construction [kən'strʌkʃn]	hier: Auslegung, Interpretation (eines Vertrags)
consultant [kən'sʌltənt]	Berater/in
consultation [ˌkɒnsl'teɪʃn]	Beratung, Besprechung
consumer price index (CPI) [kənˌsju:mə praɪs 'ɪndeks]	Verbraucherpreisindex
contract ['kɒntrækt]	Vertrag, Auftrag
contract law ['kɒntrækt lɔ:]	Vertragsrecht
contractual penalty [kənˌtræktʃuəl 'penlti]	Vertragsstrafe
to **contribute** [kən'trɪbju:t]	(Geld) beisteuern, einbringen, zuschießen
contribution [ˌkɒntrɪ'bju:ʃn]	Kapitaleinlage
to **copycat** ['kɒpikæt]	kopieren, nachahmen
copyright ['kɒpiraɪt]	Urheberrecht(e)
core business ['kɔ: bɪznəs]	Kerngeschäft
core hours ['kɔ: aʊəz]	Kernzeit
corporate ['kɔ:pərət]	Unternehmens-
corporate client [ˌkɔ:pərət 'klaɪənt]	Firmenkunde
corporation [ˌkɔ:pə'reɪʃn]	Unternehmen
counsellor ['kaʊnsələ]	Anwalt, Rechtsbeistand
court appointment ['kɔ:t əpɔɪntmənt]	Gerichtstermin
court of exchequer (UK) [ˌkɔ:t əv ɪks'tʃekə]	Finanzgericht
to **cover** ['kʌvə]	abdecken, decken
creditor ['kredɪtə]	Gläubiger
criminal offence [ˌkrɪmɪnl ə'fens]	Straftat, strafbare Handlung
to **cross-subsidise** [ˌkrɒs 'sʌbsɪdaɪz]	quersubventionieren
current expenditure [ˌkʌrənt ɪk'spendɪtʃə]	laufende Kosten
custom ['kʌstəm]	Gewohnheit, Gepflogenheit
custom-built ['kʌstəmbɪlt]	maßgefertigt
to **cut jobs** [ˌkʌt 'dʒɒbz]	Stellen abbauen

D

damages ['dæmɪdʒɪz]	Schadenersatz
damages claim ['dæmɪdʒɪz kleɪm]	Schadenersatzklage
debt counselling ['det kaʊnsəlɪŋ]	Schuldnerberatung
debt restructuring ['det ri:strʌktʃərɪŋ]	Umschuldung
deductions [dɪ'dʌkʃnz]	Abgaben
deed of partnership [ˌdi:d əv 'pɑ:tnəʃɪp]	Gesellschaftsvertrag
to **default on payment** [dɪˌfɔ:lt ɒn 'peɪmənt]	Zahlungsverpflichtungen nicht nachkommen
defective [dɪ'fektɪv]	schadhaft, fehlerhaft
defendant [dɪ'fendənt]	Beklagte/r, Angeklagte/r
delivery schedule [dɪˌlɪvəri 'ʃedju:l]	Lieferplan
demand, on ~ [ɒn dɪ'mɑ:nd]	auf Verlangen
demise [dɪ'maɪz]	Ende, Kollaps
to **demonstrate** ['demənstreɪt]	nachweisen
Department for Work and Pensions [dɪˌpɑ:tmənt fə ˌwɜ:k ən 'penʃnz]	Britisches Ministerium für Arbeit und Renten
to **deplete** [dɪ'pli:t]	vermindern, verringern
to **deposit** [dɪ'pɒzɪt]	einzahlen, anzahlen
design right [dɪ'zaɪn raɪt]	Geschmacksmuster
detrimental, to **be ~ to sb/sth** [ˌdetrɪ'mentl]	jdm/einer Sache abträglich sein
director [də'rektə]	Geschäftsführer/in
disabled access [dɪsˌeɪbld 'ækses]	Behindertenzugang
to **discipline sb** ['dɪsəplɪn]	jdn maßregeln, jdn bestrafen
discriminatory [dɪ'skrɪmɪnətəri]	diskriminierend
to **dispatch** [dɪ'spætʃ]	versenden
disposable [dɪ'spəʊzəbl]	Einweg-, Wegwerf-
dispute [dɪ'spju:t]	Streit, Streitigkeit
dissolution [ˌdɪsə'lu:ʃn]	Auflösung
distinct [dɪ'stɪŋkt]	deutlich
distinctive [dɪ'stɪŋktɪv]	besonders, unverwechselbar
distinguished [dɪs'tɪŋgwɪʃt]	angesehen, namhaft
doctor's note [ˌdɒktəz 'nəʊt]	ärztliches Attest
to **donate** [dəʊ'neɪt]	spenden
down payment ['daʊn ˌpeɪmənt]	Anzahlung
downturn ['daʊntɜ:n]	(Wirtschaft:) Flaute
draft [drɑ:ft]	Entwurf
to **draft** [drɑ:ft]	(Vertrag etc.) entwerfen, aufsetzen
to **drag on** [ˌdræg 'ɒn]	sich hinziehen
drain on finances [ˌdreɪn ən 'faɪnænsɪz]	finanzielle Belastung
to **draw up** [ˌdrɔ: 'ʌp]	(Vertrag) aufsetzen, aufstellen
due [dju:]	fällig
duress, to **act under ~** [dju'res]	unter Zwang handeln
duties ['dju:tiz]	Aufgaben

E

edge, to **give sb the ~ over sb** [edʒ]	jdm gegenüber jdm einen Vorsprung/Vorteil verschaffen
effect, to **that ~** [ɪ'fekt]	dahingehend
effect, with ~ from [ɪ'fekt]	mit Wirkung vom
effective [ɪ'fektɪv]	wirksam
efficiency [ɪ'fɪʃnsi]	Effizienz
embodiment [ɪm'bɒdɪmənt]	Verkörperung
employment [ɪm'plɔɪmənt]	Beschäftigung, Anstellung
employment law [ɪm'plɔɪmənt lɔ:]	Arbeitsrecht
employment lawyer [ɪm'plɔɪmənt lɔ:jə]	Anwalt für Arbeitsrecht

employment legislation [ɪm,plɔɪmənt ,ledʒɪs'leɪʃn]	Arbeitsgesetzgebung
to **endeavour** [ɪn'devə]	sich bemühen
to **enforce** [ɪn'fɔ:s]	durchsetzen, geltend machen, einklagen
enforceable [ɪn'fɔ:səbl]	durchsetzbar, einklagbar
to **engage in sth** [ɪn'geɪdʒ ɪn]	(Geschäfte) eingehen
to **enter (into a register)** ['entə]	(in ein Register) eintragen
to **enter (into an agreement)** ['entə]	(einen Vertrag) abschließen
enterprise ['entəpraɪz]	Unternehmen, Unternehmung
to **entitle sb to sth** [ɪn'taɪtl]	jdn zu etw berechtigen
entitled, to **be ~ to sth** [ɪn'taɪtld]	auf etw Anspruch/Recht haben
entitlement [ɪn'taɪtlmənt]	Anspruch
entrepreneur [,ɒntrəprə'nɜ:]	Unternehmer/in
entry (in a register) ['entri]	Eintrag (in ein Register)
equity ['ekwəti]	Eigenkapital
essence, of the ~ ['esns]	wesentlich
to **exceed (a date)** [ɪk'si:d]	(ein Datum) überschreiten
excessive [ɪk'sesɪv]	übertrieben
exchange rate [ɪks'tʃeɪndʒ reɪt]	Wechselkurs
exclusive rights/exclusivity [ɪks,klu:sɪv 'raɪts/ɪksklu:'sɪvəti]	Exklusivrechte
executive board [ɪg'zekjətɪv ,bɔ:d]	Vorstand
to **exercise (rights)** ['eksəsaɪz]	(Rechte) ausüben
exhibition [,eksɪ'bɪʃn]	Messe
expenses [ɪk'spensɪz]	Kosten, Aufwendungen
expert ['ekspɜ:t]	Gutachter (bei Gericht)
to **expire** [ɪk'spaɪə]	(Vertrag:) auslaufen
expiry [ɪk'spaɪəri]	Ablauf
expiry date [ɪk'spaɪəri ,deɪt]	Ablaufdatum
to **exploit** [ɪk'splɔɪt]	verwerten
exploratory talks [ɪk,splɒrətri: 'tɔ:ks]	Sondierungsgespräche
exposure [ɪk'spəʊʒə]	Risiko
exposure to risk [ɪk,spəʊʒə tə 'rɪsk]	Risikoanfälligkeit
express [ɪk'spres]	ausdrücklich
extraordinary general meeting [ɪk,strɔ:dnri,dʒenrəl 'mi:tɪŋ]	außerordentliche Hauptversammlung

F

to **fail to do sth** [feɪl]	es versäumen, etw zu tun
failure ['feɪljə]	Versäumnis; Konkurs
failure to comply [,feɪljə tə kəm'plaɪ]	Nichtbeachtung
fair dealing [,feə 'di:lɪŋ]	Kulanz(regelung)
fake [feɪk]	Fälschung, Nachahmung
fault [fɔ:lt]	Schuld
fee [fi:]	Vergütung, Honorar
to **fend sth off** [,fend 'ɒf]	etw abwehren
to **file sth with sb** [faɪl]	etw bei jdm einreichen
financial year [faɪ,nænʃl 'jɪə]	Geschäftsjahr, Rechnungsjahr
to **find common ground** [faɪnd ,kɒmən 'graʊnd]	zueinander finden
findings ['faɪndɪŋz]	Ergebnisse
fine [faɪn]	Geldstrafe, Geldbuße
fitted ['fɪtɪd]	(Kleidung:) eng, auf Figur geschnitten
flat hunting ['flæt hʌntɪŋ]	Wohnungssuche
floating charge [,fləʊtɪŋ 'tʃɑ:dʒ]	schwebende Belastung
flour ['flaʊə]	Mehl
flour mill ['flaʊə mɪl]	Kornmühle, Getreidemühle
force, in ~ [ɪn 'fɔ:s]	in Kraft
force majeure [,fɔ:s mæ'ʒɜ:]	höhere Gewalt
foreseeability [fɔ:si:ə'bɪləti]	Vorhersehbarkeit
founder ['faʊndə]	Gründer/in
freelancer ['fri:lɑ:nsə]	Freiberufler/in, Selbständige/r
to **fulfil (an obligation)** [fʊl'fɪl]	(eine Verpflichtung) erfüllen
funds [fʌndz]	Geldmittel, Kapital

G

gardening leave ['gɑ:dnɪŋ li:v]	Freistellung bei vollem Gehalt
gender stereotyping [,dʒendə 'steriətaɪpɪŋ]	klischeehafte Zuordnung der Geschlechterrollen
general partner [,dʒenrəl 'pɑ:tnə]	Komplementär/in
to **give rise to** [gɪv 'raɪz tə]	zu etw führen
to **go public** [,gəʊ 'pʌblɪk]	an die Börse gehen
to **go under** [,gəʊ 'ʌndə]	pleite gehen
to **govern** ['gʌvn]	bestimmen, regeln
to **grant sb sth** [grɑ:nt]	jdm etw gewähren
gross [grəʊs]	brutto
growth [grəʊθ]	Wachstum
growth potential ['grəʊθ pə,tenʃl]	Wachstumspotential
guarantee [,gærən'ti:]	Bürgschaft, Kaution

H

to **hail sth as sth** [heɪl]	etw als etw feiern
headquarters [,hed'kwɔ:təz]	Zentrale
hereby [,hɪə'baɪ]	hiermit
hereinafter [,hɪərɪn'ɑ:ftə]	im Folgenden
hindrance ['hɪndrəns]	Verhinderung
hostile ['hɒstaɪl]	feindlich
hug [hʌg]	Umarmung
Human Resources (HR) [,hju:mən rɪ'sɔ:sɪz]	Personal(abteilung)

I

immediate relatives [ɪ,mi:diət 'relətɪvz]	nächste Verwandte
immediate, with ~ effect [ɪ'mi:diət]	mit sofortiger Wirkung
impact ['ɪmpækt]	Auswirkung
impartial [ɪm'pɑ:ʃl]	unparteiisch
impending [ɪm'pendɪŋ]	drohend
to **implement (a measure)** ['ɪmplɪmənt]	(eine Maßnahme) umsetzen, durchführen
implication [,ɪmplɪ'keɪʃn]	Konsequenz, Auswirkung
to **impose** [ɪm'pəʊz]	(Strafe etc.) verhängen, anordnen
impractical [ɪm'præktɪkl]	nicht praktikabel
in lieu of [ɪn 'lu: əv]	anstelle von, anstatt
in-house [,ɪn 'haʊs]	hauseigen, firmenintern
incentive [ɪn'sentɪv]	Anreiz
inconsistency [,ɪnkən'sɪstənsi]	Unregelmäßigkeit
inconvenience [,ɪnkən'vi:niəns]	Unannehmlichkeit(en)
incorrect [,ɪnkə'rekt]	unsachgemäß, fehlerhaft
to **incur** [ɪn'kɜ:]	(Schulden) machen, (Unkosten) haben
to **indemnify** [ɪn'demnɪfaɪ]	entschädigen, absichern
industrial application [ɪn,dʌstriəl æplɪ'keɪʃn]	gewerbliche Verwertung, industrielle Eignung
ineffective [,ɪnɪ'fektɪv]	unwirksam, rechtsunwirksam
to **infringe (rights)** [ɪn'frɪndʒ]	(Rechte) verletzen
infringement [ɪn'frɪndʒmənt]	Rechtsverletzung, Verstoß
inheritable [ɪn'herɪtəbl]	vererbbar
injunction [ɪn'dʒʌŋkʃn]	richterliche Anordnung, einstweilige Verfügung
Inland Revenue (UK) [,ɪnlænd 'revənju]	Fiskus, Finanzamt
inoperative [ɪn'ɒpərətɪv]	rechtsunwirksam, ungültig
insider dealing [,ɪnsaɪdə 'di:lɪŋ]	Insidergeschäfte, -handel
insider information [ɪn,saɪdə ɪnfə'meɪʃn]	Insiderwissen
insolvency [ɪn'sɒlvənsi]	Insolvenz
insolvency estate [ɪn'sɒlvənsi ɪsteɪt]	Konkursmasse
insolvency law [ɪn'sɒlvənsi lɔ:]	Insolvenzrecht
insolvency practitioner [ɪn'sɒlvənsi præktɪʃənə]	Insolvenzverwalter/in
to **inspect** [ɪn'spekt]	überprüfen, inspizieren, einsehen
instalment [ɪn'stɔ:lmənt]	Rate
intellectual property [ɪntə,lektʃʊəl 'prɒpəti]	geistiges Eigentum
intellectual property rights [ɪntə,lektʃʊəl 'prɒpəti raɪts]	geistige Eigentumsrechte
intention [ɪn'tenʃn]	Absicht
intermediary [,ɪntə'mi:diəri]	Mittelsmann, Vermittler
to **intervene** [,ɪntə'vi:n]	einschreiten, eingreifen
invalid [ɪn'vælɪd]	ungültig
invoice ['ɪnvɔɪs]	Rechnung
to **invoke sth** [ɪn'vəʊk]	sich auf etw berufen
involvement [ɪn'vɒlvmənt]	Engagement, Beteiligung
issue ['ɪʃu:]	Frage, Punkt, Problem; (Aktien:) Emission
to **issue (shares)** ['ɪʃu:]	(Aktien) ausgeben, emittieren

J

job interview ['dʒɒb ɪntəvju:]	Vorstellungsgespräch
jurisdiction [,dʒʊərɪs'dɪkʃn]	Gerichtsstand, Zuständigkeitsbereich eines Gerichts

K

keeping, to **be out of ~ with sth** [ˌaʊt əv ˈkiːpɪŋ] — einer Sache nicht entsprechen
knight [naɪt] — Ritter
knock-down price [ˌnɒk daʊn ˈpraɪs] — stark reduzierter Preis

L

labelling norms [ˈleɪbəlɪŋ nɔːmz] — Kennzeichnungsrichtlinien
landlord [ˈlændlɔːd] — Vermieter
law firm [ˈlɔː fɜːm] — Anwaltskanzlei
to **lay off sb** [ˌleɪ ˈɒf] — jdn betriebsbedingt kündigen
lease [liːs] — Miete, Mietverhältnis, Pachtvertrag
leasehold agreement [ˈliːshəʊld əgriːmənt] — Pacht-, Mietvertrag
leave [liːv] — Urlaub
leave entitlement [ˈliːv ɪnˌtaɪtlmənt] — Urlaubsanspruch
legal force [ˌliːgl ˈfɔːs] — Rechtswirksamkeit, Gültigkeit
legal recourse [ˌliːgl rɪˈkɔːs] — Regressanspruch
legal scholar [ˌliːgl ˈskɒlə] — Rechtsgelehrte/r
legal structure [ˌliːgl ˈstrʌktʃə] — Rechtsform
legally effective [ˌliːgəli ɪˈfektɪv] — rechtswirksam
legislation [ˌledʒɪsˈleɪʃn] — Gesetzgebung, Recht, Gesetz
lending standards [ˈlendɪŋ stændədz] — Kreditvergaberichtlinien
lessee [leˈsiː] — Mieter/in
lessor [leˈsɔː] — Vermieter/in
to **let** [let] — vermieten
letter of intent (LOI) [ˌletər əv ɪnˈtent] — geschäftliche Verpflichtungserklärung
letting [ˈletɪŋ] — Vermietung
level of involvement [ˌlevl əv ɪnˈvɒlvmənt] — Beteiligungsgrad
leverage financing [ˈliːvərɪdʒ faɪnænsɪŋ] — Finanzierung durch Fremdkapital
liability [ˌlaɪəˈbɪləti] — Haftung, Haftbarkeit
liability insurance [ˌlaɪəˈbɪləti ɪnʃʊərəns] — Haftpflichtversicherung
liable, to **be ~ for sb/for sth** [ˈlaɪəbl] — gegenüber jdm/für etw haften
licence area [ˈlaɪsns eəriə] — Lizenzgebiet
licensee [laɪsənˈsiː] — Lizenznehmer/in
licensing agreement [ˈlaɪsnsɪŋ əgriːmənt] — Lizenzvertrag
to **lie idle** [ˌlaɪ ˈaɪdl] — stillstehen
life [laɪf] — hier: Gültigkeitsdauer (eines Vertrags)
to **lift** *(slang)* [lɪft] — klauen
to **limit** [ˈlɪmɪt] — begrenzen, beschränken
limited partner [ˌlɪmɪtɪd ˈpɑːtnə] — Kommanditist
line manager [laɪn ˈmænɪdʒə] — direkte/r Vorgesetzte/r
liquidation [ˌlɪkwɪˈdeɪʃn] — Abwicklung, Liquidation
liquidator [ˈlɪkwɪdeɪtə] — Insolvenzverwalter/in
litigation [ˌlɪtɪˈgeɪʃn] — Rechtsstreit, Klage
live-in boyfriend [lɪvˌɪn ˈbɔɪfrend] — Lebensgefährte
loan capital [ˌləʊn ˈkæpɪtl] — Fremdkapital, Anleihekapital
loan repayment [ˈləʊn rɪpeɪmənt] — Darlehensrückzahlung
loophole [ˈluːphəʊl] — Hintertür, Schlupfloch
loose [luːs] — (Kleidung:) weit (geschnitten)
to **lose out** [ˌluːz ˈaʊt] — schlecht wegkommen
loss [lɒs] — Verlust
lump-sum amount [ˌlʌmp sʌm əˈmaʊt] — Pauschalbetrag
lyrics [ˈlɪrɪks] — Songtext

M

to **make use of sth** [meɪk ˈjuːs əv] — sich einer Sache bedienen
malfunction [ˌmælˈfʌŋkʃn] — Defekt, technische Störung
managing agent [ˌmænɪdʒɪŋ ˈeɪdʒənt] — Verwalter/in, Hausverwalter/in
managing partner [ˌmænɪdʒɪŋ ˈpɑːtnə] — geschäftsführende/r Gesellschafter/in
market research [ˌmɑːkɪt rɪˈsɜːtʃ] — Marktforschung
market share [ˌmɑːkɪt ˈʃeə] — Marktanteil
measure [ˈmeʒə] — Maßnahme
memorandum of association [memәˌrændəm əv əˌsəʊsiˈeɪʃn] — Gesellschaftsvertrag
merger [ˈmɜːdʒə] — Fusion
misrepresentation [ˌmɪsreprɪzenˈteɪʃn] — Falschdarstellung
momentous [məˈmentəs] — bedeutend, folgenschwer
mortgage [ˈmɔːgɪdʒ] — Hypothek
mundane [mʌnˈdeɪn] — banal, alltäglich
mutual [ˈmjuːtʃuəl] — gegenseitig

N

nappy (BE) [ˈnæpi] — Windel
natural disaster [ˌnætʃrəl dɪˈzɑːstə] — Naturkatastrophe
to **necessitate** [nəˈsesɪteɪt] — erforderlich machen
negotiation [nɪˌgəʊʃiˈeɪʃn] — Verhandlung
net [net] — netto, Netto-
non-disclosure agreement (NDA) [nɒn dɪsˌkləʊʒə əˈgriːmənt] — Geheimhaltungsvereinbarung
non-voting stock [ˈnɒnvəʊtɪŋ stɒk] — Aktie ohne Stimmrecht
notary [ˈnəʊtəri] — Notar
notice period [ˌnəʊtɪs ˈpɪəriəd] — Kündigungsfrist
notification [ˌnəʊtɪfɪˈkeɪʃn] — Meldung
to **notify** [ˈnəʊtɪfaɪ] — benachrichtigen, mitteilen, melden
notwithstanding [ˌnɒtwɪθˈstændɪŋ] — unbeschadet
novel [ˈnɒvl] — Roman
null and void [ˌnʌl ən ˈvɔɪd] — null und nichtig

O

object of the company [ˌɒbdʒɪkt əv ðə ˈkʌmpəni] — Gegenstand des Unternehmens
obligation [ˌɒblɪˈgeɪʃn] — (Vertrag:) Verpflichtung; (Finanzen:) Verbindlichkeit
obliged, to **be ~ to sth** [əˈblaɪdʒd] — zu etw verpflichtet sein
to **obtain sth** [əbˈteɪn] — etw erhalten
obviousness [ˈɒbviəsnəs] — (Patentrecht:) mangelnde Erfindungshöhe
offence [əˈfens] — Vergehen, Delikt, Straftat
Office of Fair Trading [ˌɒfɪs əv feə ˈtreɪdɪŋ] — britisches Kartellamt, Amt für Verbraucherschutz
to **offload goods** [ɒfˌləʊd gʊdz] — Ware abstoßen
operating costs [ˈɒpəreɪtɪŋ kɒsts] — Betriebskosten
operation [ˌɒpəˈreɪʃn] — Betrieb
ordinary partnership [ˌɔːdnri ˈpɑːtnəʃɪp] — Offene Handelsgesellschaft (OHG)
out-of-court settlement [ˌaʊt əv kɔːt ˈsetlmənt] — außergerichtliche Einigung
outcome [ˈaʊtkʌm] — Ergebnis
to **over-expose oneself** [ˌəʊvərɪkˈspəʊz] — sich einem zu hohen Verlustrisiko aussetzen
overdraft [ˈəʊvədrɑːft] — Überziehungskredit
to **overstate** [ˌəʊvəˈsteɪt] — zu hoch ansetzen
to **overstretch** [əʊvəˈstretʃ] — überfordern
overtime account [ˈəʊvətaɪm əkaʊnt] — Überstundenkonto
owner [ˈəʊnə] — Inhaber/in, Eigentümer/in

P

paid up [ˌpeɪd ˈʌp] — (Kapitaleinlage:) (voll) eingezahlt
panel [ˈpænl] — Gremium
participation [pɑːˌtɪsɪˈpeɪʃn] — Beteiligung
partnership [ˈpɑːtnəʃɪp] — (Personen-)Gesellschaft
partnership agreement [ˈpɑːtnəʃɪp əgriːmənt] — Gesellschaftsvertrag
party to a contract [ˌpɑːti tʊ ə ˈkɒntrækt] — Vertragspartei
to **pass a resolution** [ˌpɑːs ə reʒəˈluːʃn] — einen Beschluss fassen
passing off [ˌpɑːsɪŋ ˈɒf] — Warenzeichenmissbrauch
patentee [peɪtənˈtiː] — Patentinhaber
to **pave the way for sth** [peɪv ðə ˈweɪ] — einer Sache den Weg ebnen
pay [peɪ] — Lohn, Gehalt
payable [ˈpeɪəbl] — zahlbar
payment period [ˈpeɪmənt pɪəriəd] — Zahlungsfrist
penalty [ˈpenəlti] — Strafe, Konventionalstrafe
pension scheme (BE) [ˈpenʃn skiːm] — betriebliche Altersversorgung
to **perform (an agreement)** [pəˈfɔːm] — (einen Vertrag) erfüllen
performance [pəˈfɔːməns] — (Vertrags-)Erfüllung, Leistung
performance bonus [pəˈfɔːməns bəʊnəs] — Leistungsprämie
performing fee [pəˈfɔːmɪŋ fiː] — Lizenzgebühr, GEMA-Gebühr
permitted [pəˈmɪtɪd] — zugelassen
perpetuity, in ~ [ɪn ˌpɜːpəˈtjuːəti] — auf Dauer
personal assets [ˌpɜːsənl ˈæsets] — Privatvermögen

plaintiff ['pleɪntɪf]	Kläger/in
plant and equipment [,plɑ:nt ənd ɪ'kwɪpmənt]	Maschinen und Anlagen
to **poach staff** [,pəʊtʃ 'stɑ:f]	Personal abwerben
to **practise** ['præktɪs]	praktizieren
preamble [prɪ'æmbl]	Präambel
precaution [prɪ'kɔ:ʃn]	Vorsichtsmaßnahme
predictable [prɪ'dɪktəbl]	vorhersehbar, vorhersagbar
preferential creditor [prefə,renʃl 'kredɪtə]	bevorzugte/r Gläubiger/in
premises ['premɪsɪz]	Geschäftsräume
premium ['pri:miəm]	Aufpreis
presence ['prezns]	Anwesenheit
price fixing ['praɪs fɪksɪŋ]	Preisabsprache
principal place of business [,prɪnsəpl ,pleɪs əv 'bɪznəs]	Hauptgeschäftssitz
priority date [praɪ'ɒrəti deɪt]	Prioritätsdatum
probationary period [prə,beɪʃnri 'pɪəriəd]	Probezeit
procedure(s) [prə'si:dʒəz]	Verfahren
to **proceed** [prə'si:d]	verfahren
proceeds ['prəʊsi:dz]	Erlös, Einkünfte
to **produce (a document)** [prə'dju:s]	(ein Dokument) vorlegen
productivity [,prɒdʌk'tɪvəti]	Produktivität
profession [prə'feʃn]	Beruf, Berufsstand, Metier
profit allocation ['prɒfɪt æləkeɪʃn]	Gewinnverteilung
proof of debt [,pru:f əv 'det]	Nachweis einer Forderung
proofreading ['pru:fri:dɪŋ]	Korrekturlesen
property (BE) ['prɒpəti]	Immobilien
prosecution [,prɒsɪ'kju:ʃn]	Strafverfolgung
prospective [prə'spektɪv]	potentiell
to **prove one's case** [,pru:v wʌnz 'keɪs]	überzeugende Beweise erbringen
provision [prə'vɪʒn]	Bestimmung
proxy ['prɒksi]	Bevollmächtigte/r
public domain [,pʌblɪk də'meɪn]	öffentlich
publishing house ['pʌblɪʃɪŋ haʊs]	Verlag
purchaser ['pɜ:tʃəsə]	Käufer/in
pursuant to [pə'sju:ənt tə]	in Übereinstimmung mit, entsprechend, gemäß
to **put up capital** [,pʊt ʌp 'kæpɪtl]	Kapital bereitstellen, aufbringen

Q

quality assurance ['kwɒləti ə,ʃʊərəns]	Qualitätssicherung
quarterly ['kwɔ:təli]	vierteljährlich

R

to **raise (an issue)** [reɪz]	(eine Frage) aufwerfen, (ein Problem) anschneiden
to **raise (capital)** [reɪz]	(Kapital) aufbringen, beschaffen
random sampling [,rændəm 'sɑ:mplɪŋ]	Stichprobe(n)
range of products [,reɪndʒ əv 'prɒdʌkts]	Produktpalette, Sortiment
rate of interest [,reɪt əv 'ɪntrəst]	Zinssatz
ratio ['reɪʃiəʊ]	Verhältnis
rationale [,ræʃə'nɑ:l]	Begründung, Hintergründe
real estate (AE) ['rɪəl ɪsteɪt]	Immobilien
to **realize assets** [,rɪəlaɪz 'æsets]	Vermögen veräußern
reason, by ~ of ['ri:zn]	aufgrund
reasonableness ['ri:znəblnəs]	Verhältnismäßigkeit
recall [rɪ'kɔ:l]	Rückruf
receipt [rɪ'si:t]	hier: Erhalt
receipts [rɪ'si:ts]	Einkünfte
reconcileable [,rekən'saɪləbl]	vereinbar
to **recover sth** [rɪ'kʌvə]	etw zurückbekommen
redevelopment [,ri:dɪ'veləpmənt]	Sanierung
redundancy [rɪ'dʌndənsi]	betriebsbedingte Kündigung
redundancy clause [rɪ'dʌndənsi klɔ:z]	Kündigungsklausel
refastenable [ri:'fɑ:snəbl]	wiederverschließbar
regarding [rɪ'gɑ:dɪŋ]	betreffend, bezüglich
register of companies [,redʒɪstər əv 'kʌmpəniz]	Gesellschaftsregister, Handelsregister
regulation [,regju'leɪʃn]	Regulierung
to **reject** [rɪ'dʒekt]	ablehnen
rejection [rɪ'dʒekʃn]	Ablehnung
release [rɪ'li:s]	Veröffentlichung, Erscheinen
relevant ['reləvənt]	entsprechend
remittance [rɪ'mɪtns]	Überweisung
remuneration (BE) [rɪ,mju:nə'reɪʃn]	Entgelt, Vergütung
to **render (null and void)** ['rendə]	(null und nichtig) machen
to **renegotiate** [,ri: nɪ'gəʊʃieɪt]	neu verhandeln
rent [rent]	Miete
rental income ['rentl ɪnkʌm]	Mieteinkünfte
to **report for duty** [rɪ,pɔ:t fə 'dju:ti]	zum Dienst erscheinen
to **represent sb** [,reprɪ'zent]	jdn vertreten
representative [,reprɪ'zentətɪv]	Vertreter/in
reprisal [rɪ'praɪzl]	Repressalie
required [rɪ'kwaɪəd]	erforderlich
requirement [rɪ'kwaɪəmənt]	Voraussetzung, Bedingung, Bestimmung
Research and Development (R&D) [rɪ,sɜ:tʃ ən dɪ'veləpmənt]	Forschung und Entwicklung(sabteilung)
residence permit [,rezɪdəns 'pɜ:mɪt]	Aufenthaltserlaubnis
to **resign (from a job)** [rɪ'zaɪn]	(eine Anstellung) kündigen
resignation [,rezɪg'neɪʃn]	Kündigung
resolution [,rezə'lu:ʃn]	Beschluss
to **restrict sth** [rɪ'strɪkt]	etw beschränken, einschränken, begrenzen
restriction [rɪ'strɪkʃn]	Einschränkung, Beschränkung
revenue ['revənju:]	Einkünfte, Einnahmen
to **revert to sb** [rɪ'vɜ:t]	(Rechte) auf jdn zurückfallen
right of audience [,raɪt əv 'ɔ:diəns]	Zulassung eines Anwalts bei einem Gericht
to **ring in sick** [rɪŋ ,ɪn 'sɪk]	sich (telefonisch) krank melden
rip-off ['rɪpɒf]	Abzockerei
risk assessment ['rɪsk əsesmənt]	Risikoabschätzung, -bewertung
risk, at ~ [ət 'rɪsk]	gefährdet
risk management [rɪsk 'mænɪdʒmənt]	Risikomanagement
royalties ['rɔɪəltiz]	Tantiemen
ruling ['ru:lɪŋ]	Entscheidung, Beschluss

S

safeguard ['seɪfgɑ:d]	Schutzmaßnahme
safety inspection ['seɪfti ɪnspekʃn]	Sicherheitsüberprüfung
salary ['sæləri]	Gehalt
savings ['seɪvɪŋz]	Einsparungen
to **schedule** ['ʃedju:l]	planen, festlegen
scope [skəʊp]	Spielraum, Umfang
screening process ['skri:nɪŋ prəʊses]	Auswahl-, Prüfverfahren
to **secure sth** [sɪ'kjʊə]	etw erhalten, bekommen
to **secure sth against sth** [sɪ'kjʊə]	etw gegen etw absichern
secured creditor [sɪ,kjʊəd 'kredɪtə]	gesicherte/r Gläubiger/in
self-employed [,self ɪm'plɔɪd]	selbständig
separability clause (AE) [,seprə'bɪləti ,klɔ:z]	salvatorische Klausel
seriousness ['sɪəriəsnəs]	Ernsthaftigkeit
to **serve notice** [,sɜ:v 'nəʊtɪs]	die Kündigung einreichen
to **service debts** [,sɜ:vɪs 'dets]	Zins- und Tilgungszahlungen leisten
services ['sɜ:vɪsɪz]	Dienstleistungen
to **set forth** [,set 'fɔ:θ]	dartun, niederlegen, darlegen
to **set sth out** [,set 'aʊt]	etw darlegen
severance clause (BE) ['sevərəns ,klɔ:z]	salvatorische Klausel
shaft [ʃɑ:ft]	Achse
share [ʃeə]	Aktie, Anteil
share capital ['ʃeə kæpɪtl]	Aktienkapital
share issue ['ʃeər ɪʃu:]	Aktienemission
share price ['ʃeə praɪs]	Aktienkurs
shareholder ['ʃeəhəʊldə]	Teilhaber/in, Gesellschafter/in, Aktionär/in
shareholding ['ʃeəhəʊldɪŋ]	Anteil, Beteiligung
to **sharpen sth up** [,ʃɑ:pən 'ʌp]	etw aufpolieren, verbessern
shelf company ['ʃelf kʌmpəni]	Mantelgesellschaft
sick note ['sɪk nəʊt]	Krankmeldung
sickness ['sɪknəs]	Krankheit, Erkrankung

social insurance [ˌsəʊʃl ɪn'ʃʊərəns]	Sozialversicherung
sole proprietorship [ˌsəʊl prə'praɪətəʃɪp]	Einzelunternehmen
sole trader [ˌsəʊl 'treɪdə]	Einzelunternehmer/in
solicitor (BE) [sə'lɪsɪtə]	Anwalt/Anwältin
sound [saʊnd]	solide
spare [speə]	Ersatz
special leave [ˌspeʃl 'li:v]	Sonderurlaub
specifications [ˌspesɪfɪ'keɪʃnz]	technische Daten, Angaben
to **specify** ['spesɪfaɪ]	angeben, vorschreiben
speculative ['spekjuleɪtɪv]	spekulativ
spouse [spaʊz]	Gatte/Gattin
spreadsheet ['spredʃi:t]	Tabellenkalkulation
stake [steɪk]	Anteil
stamp [stæmp]	Stempel, (Gebühren-)Marke
statement ['steɪtmənt]	(Finanzen:) Abrechnung
statute, provided for by ~ ['stætʃu:t]	gesetzlich vorgesehen
statutory ['stætʃətri]	gesetzlich
steam engine ['sti:m endʒɪn]	Dampfmaschine
to **stipulate** ['stɪpjuleɪt]	festlegen, festsetzen, vorschreiben
strength, on the ~ of sth ['streŋθ]	aufgrund einer Sache
stringent ['strɪndʒənt]	streng
sub-contractor [ˌsʌbkən'træktə]	Subunternehmer/in, Zulieferer/in
to **submit** [səb'mɪt]	einreichen
subsidiary [səb'sɪdiəri]	Tochterunternehmen, -gesellschaft
successor [sək'sesə]	Rechtsnachfolger
to **sue** [su:]	klagen, Klage erheben
to **sue sb** [su:]	jdn verklagen
to **summon sb to appear in court** ['sʌmən]	jdn vor Gericht laden
supervisory board [su:pə'vaɪsəri bɔ:d]	Aufsichtsrat
supplier [sə'plaɪə]	Lieferant/in
supply [sə'plaɪ]	Lieferung
surplus ['sɜ:pləs]	Überschuss
to **surrender sth** [sə'rendə]	etw überlassen, auf etw verzichten
to **surrender sth to sb** [sə'rendə]	jdm etw übergeben

T

to **take over (a company)** [ˌteɪk 'əʊvə]	(ein Unternehmen) übernehmen
takeover ['teɪkəʊvə]	Übernahme
takeover bid ['teɪkəʊvə bɪd]	Übernahmeangebot
tangible assets [ˌtændʒəbl 'æsets]	Sachvermögen, Sachwerte
to **target sth** ['tɑ:gɪt]	etw ins Visier nehmen
target company ['tɑ:gɪt kʌmpəni]	Übernahmekandidat
tax adviser ['tæks ədvaɪzə]	Steuerberater/in
tax burden ['tæks bɜ:dn]	Steuerlast
tax office ['tæks ɒfɪs]	Finanzamt
tax status ['tæks steɪtəs]	Steuerstatus
technical term [ˌteknɪkl 'tɜ:m]	Fachbegriff, Fachausdruck
tentative ['tentətɪv]	zaghaft, tastend
term of employment [ˌtɜ:m əv ɪm'plɔɪmənt]	Anstellungsdauer
to **terminate sth** ['tɜ:mɪneɪt]	etw beenden, (Vertrag) auflösen, lösen
termination [ˌtɜ:mɪ'neɪʃn]	Beendigung, Ende; (Vertrag:) Auflösung
terms [tɜ:mz]	Bedingungen
terms and conditions [ˌtɜ:mz ənd kən'dɪʃnz]	(Verkaufs-, Geschäfts-) Bedingungen
terms of delivery [ˌtɜ:mz əv dɪ'lɪvəri]	Lieferbedingungen
to **testify** ['testɪfaɪ]	(als Zeuge) aussagen
testing regime [ˌtestɪŋ reɪ'ʒi:m]	Testverfahren
theft [θeft]	Diebstahl
third party [ˌθɜ:d 'pɑ:ti]	Dritter
timber processing ['tɪmbə prəʊsesɪŋ]	Holzverarbeitung
time scale ['taɪm skeɪl]	Zeitrahmen, Zeitplan
title ['taɪtl]	Eigentumsrecht
trade [treɪd]	Gewerbe(betrieb)
trade fair ['treɪd feə]	Messe
trade mark ['treɪd mɑ:k]	Warenzeichen, Marke
trade office ['treɪd ɒfɪs]	Gewerbeamt
trader ['treɪdə]	Gewerbetreibende/r
trainee lawyer [ˌtreɪni: 'lɔ:jə]	Referendar/in
transaction [træn'zækʃn]	(Geschäfts-)Vorgang
transfer ['trænsfɜ:]	Übertragung
tribunal ruling [traɪˌbju:nl 'ru:lɪŋ]	Gerichtsentscheidung
trivial ['trɪviəl]	belanglos, unwichtig
trustee [trʌ'sti:]	Treuhänder/in, Verwalter/in
turnover ['tɜ:nəʊvə]	Umsatz
tussle *(slang)* ['tʌsl]	Streit, Zoff

U

unaffected [ˌʌnə'fektɪd]	unberührt
unawares, to catch sb ~ [ˌkætʃ ʌnə'weəz]	jdn überraschen, überrumpeln
unconfirmed [ˌʌnkən'fɜ:md]	unbestätigt
to **undertake to do sth** [ˌʌndə'teɪk]	sich (dazu) verpflichten, etw zu tun
unforeseeable [ʌnfɔ:'si:əbl]	unvorhersehbar
unified ['ju:nɪfaɪd]	einheitlich
union pay rate [ˌju:niən 'peɪ reɪt]	Tariflohn
union shop steward ['ju:niən ʃɒp stju:əd]	Gewerkschaftsvertreter
unlimited [ʌn'lɪmɪtɪd]	unbeschränkt
unmistakeable [ʌnmɪ'steɪkəbl]	unverkennbar
unreasonable [ʌn'ri:znəbl]	unverhältnismäßig
unsatisfactory [ˌʌnˌsætɪs'fæktəri]	nicht zufriedenstellend, unbefriedigend
unsecured creditor [ʌnsɪˌkjuəd 'kredɪtə]	ungesicherte/r Gläubiger/in
unsuspecting [ʌnsə'spektɪŋ]	nichtsahnend, ahnungslos
usage ['ju:sɪdʒ]	Gebrauch

V

vaccination [ˌvæksɪ'neɪʃn]	Impfung
valid ['vælɪd]	gültig
validity [və'lɪdəti]	Gültigkeit
to **value sth** ['vælju:]	den Wert von etw schätzen
VAT (value added tax) [ˌvælju: 'ædɪd tæks]	Mehrwertsteuer
Velcro fastener ['velkrəʊ fɑ:snə]	Klettverschluss
venture ['ventʃə]	Unternehmen
verbal ['vɜ:bl]	mündlich
viable ['vaɪəbl]	realisierbar, durchführbar
victory ['vɪktəri]	Sieg
vis à vis [ˌvi:z ɑ: 'vi:]	gegenüber
void [vɔɪd]	nichtig, ungültig, unwirksam
voluntary ['vɒləntri]	freiwillig
voluntary redundancy (BE) [ˌvɒləntri rɪ'dʌndənsi]	freiwilliges Ausscheiden
voting stock ['vəʊtɪŋ stɒk]	Stimmrechtsaktie

W

wages ['weɪdʒɪz]	Lohn
to **waive sth** [weɪv]	auf etw verzichten
to **ward sth off** [ˌwɔ:d 'ɒf]	etw abwehren
to **warrant** ['wɒrənt]	garantieren, gewährleisten
warranty ['wɒrənti]	Garantie
warranty of title [ˌwɒrənti əv 'taɪtl]	Rechtsmängelhaftung
warranty period ['wɒrənti pɪəriəd]	Garantiefrist
wary ['weəri]	misstrauisch, vorsichtig
to **wind up (a company)** [ˌwaɪnd 'ʌp]	(ein Unternehmen) auflösen, abwickeln, liquidieren
winding-up petition [ˌwaɪndɪŋ 'ʌp pətɪʃn]	Antrag auf Liquidation
winding-up order [ˌwaɪndɪŋ 'ʌp ɔ:də]	Liquidationsbeschluss
to **wipe sth out** [ˌwaɪp 'aʊt]	etw auslöschen
to **withhold** [wɪð'həʊld]	vorenthalten, verweigern
witness ['wɪtnəs]	Zeuge/Zeugin
wording ['wɜ:dɪŋ]	Formulierung, Wortlaut
work permit ['wɜ:k pɜ:mɪt]	Arbeitserlaubnis
workforce ['wɜ:kfɔ:s]	Belegschaft
works council [ˌwɜ:ks 'kaʊnsl]	Betriebsrat
to **write sth off** [ˌraɪt 'ɒf]	etw abschreiben
writing, in ~ [ɪn 'raɪtɪŋ]	schriftlich
written notice [ˌrɪtn 'nəʊtɪs]	schriftliche Benachrichtigung

Z

zilch [zɪltʃ]	nix

Useful phrases and vocabulary

REFERRING TO A LEGAL DOCUMENT

The following expressions are useful when referring to a legal document or explaining its content:

It says in clause 3 **that** ...
The termination clause clearly **states / stipulates that** ...
According to clause 5 the employee **must** ...
It says here ... **which simply means that** ...

EXPRESSING RIGHTS AND OBLIGATIONS

Contracts often talk about **rights** and **obligations**.
Rights
The employee **is entitled / is allowed to / has the right to / can** take 30 days' leave.

Obligations

The employee **must / is required to / is obliged to / has a duty to / has to** treat all company data and files with complete confidentiality.

EXPRESSIONS COMMON IN CONTRACTS

Compound adverbs
In a preamble to a contract – this part of a contract is also called "recitals" – the words **whereas** and **whereby** can seem confusing. In general, **whereas** in this context simply introduces the information about the transaction that the two parties want to enter into and **whereby** introduces the main part of the contract in which all the agreed clauses are set out.

The difference between **hereafter** and **hereinafter** is as follows: **hereafter** means "from this point in time" and **hereinafter** – "from this point in the document". Equally, **thereafter** means "from that point in time".

In "The supplier **hereby** agrees that ..." the word **hereby** means "as a result of this document". In "The obligations **hereunder** of the supplier cannot be assigned except with ...", the word **hereunder** means "under this agreement".

Moreover, words like **hereto, thereof** and **herewith** are not as difficult as they look.

Here is used in a legal document to refer to this document.
There is used to refer to documents or agreements other than this document itself.

Depending on the context, a preposition can be added to **here** or **there**.
For example: "The parties to this agreement" can become "The parties **hereto**".
"The whole sum or any part **of** it" can become "The whole sum or any part **thereof**".

Adjective + preposition

Contracts often contain difficult adjective + preposition word pairs, like **subject to, pursuant to or conditional upon**. Basically, all three mean the same as **in accordance with**.

STYLE TIPS FOR LEGAL TEXTS

Legal English often uses **past participles** to make sentences more compact. Instead of:
"The price which is charged for the goods shall be ..." or "... the number of items which is specified in Annex 2"
The contract says:
"The price **charged** for the goods shall be ..." or "... the number of items **specified** in Annex 2"

Present participles are also used to make sentences more compact. So instead of:
"The agreement which exists between the two parties is due to expire at the end of this calendar year."
We can say:
"The agreement **existing** between the two parties is due to expire at the end of this calendar year."

INTERACTING WITH A CLIENT

Lawyers need to get information from their clients and summarize what the client has said, to direct the consultation and to express their own point of view. The following questions and expressions can be useful.

Getting information

Could I start by asking you when / why / how the problem began?
And what happened then?
What did you do then?
How did the other party react to this?
Could you explain why ...?

Getting the client to refocus

Let me take you back to .... .

Checking and clarifying

So, if I understand you correctly ...
Could you explain what you mean by ...?

Expressing an opinion

As I see it ...
Our best option would be to ...

GIVING ADVICE AND MAKING RECOMMENTDATIONS

Some expressions for giving advice and making recommendations require a gerund and some an infinitive. Note: Some phrases are appropriate when spoken but are not appropriate in a formal written context.

Gerund (-ing)

I (would / wouldn't) *suggest* / *recommend* **doing** something to limit your liability.
How / What about **doing** something to limit your liability? **(spoken)**

Infinitive

I think / don't think you *should* **allow** yourself to be liable for unlimited sums.
I (strongly) *advise* you to **limit** your liability.
You *could* always **change** the objects clause. **(spoken)**
You *ought* to **change** the objects clause. **(spoken)**
Why don't you **change** the objects clause? (**spoken**)

All the above phrases can be used when you are advising someone directly.

If you are discussing what **he** / **she** / **they** should do, you can use the following phrases:

I would (wouldn't) advise him to ...
I (don't) think we should ...
He (really) ought to ...
He could always ...

If you would like to *recommend* and *suggest* concerning a third party, the structure is as follows:

I recommend / suggest that s/he should + infinitive

GIVING REASONS AND EXPLANATIONS

It is often important to give reasons and explain things step by step.
Note: Words like **firstly** and **first of all** aren't used in the same way.

Enumerating reasons

Firstly, the investor is investing with minimum risk ...
Secondly, the investor receives 75% of any rent above the minimum.
Thirdly, ...
Finally, ...

Explaining the steps involved in a procedure

First of all, we need to discuss the business relationship between ...
Next, I would suggest depositing ...
Following that, it would be your job to persuade ...
Last of all, we would notify the tax office ...

NB. Be careful with **at first**. We use this to express the fact that we thought something initially and then changed our minds.

Example: At first it seemed to be a good idea to form a private limited company. Later we realized that this would be too expensive and too complicated.

EMPHASIZING A POINT

We can add emphasis to what we say in the following ways:

1 By stressing a particular word e.g. I ***will*** try to keep it straightforward.
2 By adding the auxiliary "do" e.g. I **did** find ...
3 By restructuring the statement, "Clause 5 is the problem" into **"It's** clause 5 **that** is the problem."
4 By restructuring the statement, "I would recommend that you allocate..." into **"What** I would recommend **is** that you allocate ..."
5 By moving certain negative or near negative adverbs or adverbial phrases e.g. **never**, **under no circumstances**, **at no time**, **on no account**, **seldom** to the beginning of the sentence.

Therefore, "You should not under any circumstances, just allow the lease to be extended" becomes **"Under no circumstances should you** just allow the lease to be extended."
When we use this structure the subject and verb invert i.e. "you should" becomes "should you".

NB When the main verb is in the *simple present* or *simple past* the following happens:
"My client never claimed he was a partner in the company" becomes "Never **did** my client **claim** he was a ..."

PRESENTING AN OUTCOME

We agreed / decided to ...
The best option here is to ...
In return they will ...
By way of compensation they will ...

HYPOTHESIZING ABOUT PAST ACTIONS

Sometimes in the legal profession it is important to look back at the past and consider possibilities that were an alternative at the time, but that didn't happen. We often do this when we talk about mistakes we made or mistakes we avoided making. The structure works as follows:

If we **hadn't implemented** those risk management measures, we **would have gone** under.

The logic of the statement is that they **did** implement the risk management measures and as a result they **didn't** go under.

LANGUAGE OF NEGOTIATION

In a negotiation, **confrontational** language ("We can't possibly accept that.") states absolutes and closes down options. **Tentative** language ("We would find that difficult to accept.") makes the speaker's position clear, but leaves options open.

Tentative

I'm afraid my board *might* find that figure a little low.
We *might be able* to agree to ... if we could participate in ...
Any other type of agreement *isn't* really *workable* ...
EUR 30,000 *isn't really* high *enough*.
I think EUR 45,000 is a *little* high.

is better than...

Confrontational

My board *will* find that figure too low.
We will agree to ... if we *can* participate in ...
Any other type of agreement is *unworkable* ...
EUR 30,000 is *too* low.
EUR 45,000 is *too* much.

MAKING COMPARISONS

When you compare, for example, laws or legal structures you can use the following phrases:

The German "BaFin"	**is (broadly, basically)**	**equivalent to** **similar to** **comparable to** **like** **the same as**	the US Securities and Exchange Commission.
	is (a little, very, completely)	**unlike** **different from**	
	differs (slightly, completely)	**from**	

WORD BULIDING – LEGAL VOCABULARY

Prefixes and suffixes are added to modify words.

Prefixes e.g. in-, un-, over-, ex-, are used to change the meaning of a word.
Suffixes e.g. -ate, -able, -tion, -ship, -ment, -ism, -ee, -ity, -ly, are used to change both the meaning and the grammar of a word, i.e. to turn it into a noun, an adjective, an adverb.

Look at the following examples:

valid (adj.) – **in**valid (adj.), valid**ity** (n), valid**ate** (v)
patent (n. or v.) – patent**ee** (n. *person*), patent**ed** (adj.), patent**able** (adj.)
compose (v.) – compose**r** (n. *person*), compos**ition** (n.)
respond (v.) – respon**se** (n.), respond**ent** (n. *person*), respon**sive** (adj.), **un**respon**sive** (adj.)

EXPRESSIONS USED IN TAKEOVERS

A lot of colourful expressions are used in the context of takeovers. Here are a few common ones.

white knight	A friendly bidder who is brought in by the target company to outbid a hostile bidder.
black knight	This is a hostile bidder.
poison pill	A strategy adopted by the target company to make itself unattractive to the bidding company. It might involve a shareholders' rights plan, changes to voting and non-voting stock, or an acquisition which burdens the target company with higher levels of debt.
killer bees	These are the experts (lawyers, accountants etc.) employed by a target company to fend off a hostile takeover bid.
whitemail	This is the opposite of blackmail. Here the target company sells stock to a friendly third party at a discount price.
bear hug	The bidder offers a share price too high to refuse.
crown jewels	All the valuable assets of the target company.

UNIT 1, page 15, Final Provisions – replies to letters

Reply 1

You do not say whether you incorporated your business as a limited company or traded as a partnership.

Many people create partnerships without intending to. Such an informal partnership is known as a "Partnership at will". Without anything in writing to the contrary, any partner may dissolve a partnership at will at any time by giving little or no notice. This appears to be what has happened.

There is a general requirement that partners act in good faith towards each other but you were both aware of your respective external projects and there does not appear to have been any bad faith, so it is unlikely you will have any claim against your former partner. However, there is a presumption (*Vermutung*) of equality in the share of any profits and conversely (*im umgekehrten Fall*), equal liability for any business losses. So you might be able to look to your former partner for an equal contribution to cover any losses.

Allan Donovan, barrister

Reply 2

Your question demonstrates the importance of making sure you purchase adequate insurance before you cease trading. The advice you have already received is broadly correct, so the claim is against the partners personally. You will need to take legal advice as to whether the claim has been made in time.

If the claim is made in time, you will need to consider whether it is covered by insurance and whether you have been indemnified against all liabilities. An indemnity of this kind should have been in the business transfer document, and this should also have dealt with the apportionment (*Verteilung*) of insured liabilities between the partnership and the company. If you feel the claim may be insured, notify the insurer straight away.

The transfer of a business to a limited liability company or limited liability partnership will provide only a degree of protection to the partners from claims being made against them personally.

Jon Sutcliffe, Partner at Kingston Smith LLP